Introduction

When this book first appeared in 1902, the United States was a very different place than it is today. In 1902 two-thirds of the nation's 76 million people lived in rural areas like Cape Cod rather than in cities. A majority of Cape Codders lived on farms as did 42 percent of all Americans—ten times the proportion who do so today. The US center of population in 1902 lay east of Indianapolis. Today it lies more than 300 miles further west, on the other side of St. Louis.

As they had throughout the 19th Century and earlier, a great many Americans in 1902 still produced most of their own food and other necessities. On a per capita basis, cash incomes were very small. The Constitutional amendment that would empower the US Congress to authorize the collection of federal income tax lay a decade in the future. The Federal Government, including the US Life-Saving Service, was funded entirely through such sources as import duties and excise taxes. The American economy was expanding. The national debt was 1.2 billion dollars—half of what it had been at the end of the Civil War—and declining. It would continue to decline until World War I. In 1902, Congress appropriated $1,742,000 for the operations of the US Life-Saving Service nationwide.

There was no National Park Service although the United States already had nine national parks, most of which were administered by the US Army.

The nation had only recently won its "splendid little war" with Spain. Vice President Theodore Roosevelt—the hero of that conflict—had succeeded President William McKinley after McKinley's tragic assasination the previous September. In this era, before radio and long before television, elected officials and other important people could be seen and heard only in person. Security measures as stringent as today's were impossible. McKinley had been greeting visitors to the Pan-American Exposition in Buffalo, New York when he became the third President of the United States to be assasinated within 36 years.

******

By 1902 the US Life-Saving Service had been in existance for thirty years. On Cape Cod it had matured into its fullest form, with thirteen stations (counting those on Monomoy Island) staffed by 120 men. Between August 8, 1901 and June 3, 1902, these Lifesavers had gone to the aid of 28 vessels in distress, had rescued 217 people, and had warned 36 other vessels from danger by signaling while on their patrols. Since Cape Cod had such a concentration of Life-saving stations, personnel, and activity, it is perhaps inevitable that the Service's District Superintendent for the 32 stations on the coast of Massachusetts should be a Cape

Codder. Benjamin C. Sparrow of Orleans had served as District Superintendent since the Service's inception in 1872. George W. Bowley, who would succeed Sparrow, was in 1902 Keeper of the Pamet River Station in Truro.

Sparrow was a long-time member of the Life-Saving Service's internal Board on Life-Saving Appliances. Under his direction, the Cape had for a number of years served as a proving ground for the testing of line-throwing devices while the Life-Saving Service pursued its unending (but ultimately fruitless) search for a line-throwing method that improved on US Army Lieutenant David Lyle's 1878 invention: a minature bronze cannon which fired a tight-fitting, two-pound projectile that resembled an oversize window-sash weight. Lyle guns became the standard of the maritime world, and were universally in service ashore and aboard ship through 1952. Their eventual replacement was the helicopter.

Cape Cod in 1902 was the scene of experimentation with another technological advance that was to improve maritime saftey dramatically, as well as leading onward to radio, radar and television. In South Wellfleet that year, Guglielmo Marconi was perfecting his wireless telegraph. Although he is remembered most for his pioneering trans-Atlantic transmissions in January 1903, his invention's greatest impact lay in its reformation of ship-to-shore and ship-to-ship communications, especially in emergencies. One of the first major demonstrations of the ability of the Marconi apparatus to reduce loss of life at sea came during the RMS *Titanic* disaster a decade later

******

Within Cape Cod National Seashore, as well as elsewhere, only a few tangible reminders of the Life-Saving Service era remain today.

Perhaps the most evocative of these is the Old Harbor Life-Saving Station. The station was nearly new in 1902, and stood on Nauset Beach at the entrance to Chatham's Old Harbor, north and east of the lighthouse and present-day Coast Guard Station. This location, equidistant between the Chatham and Orleans stations, is close to the site of the tragic wreck of the schooner *Calvin B. Orcutt* which foundered in a snowstorm on Christmas eve, 1896. The crews of both the Chatham and Orleans stations went to the aid of the vessel, but were severely hampered by weather conditions and could rescue no one. The decision to build the new station was an outcome of the investigation of this incident.

By 1977, shoreline erosion threatened to destroy the station. The National Park Service relocated it to Race Point Beach in Provincetown and situated it so that it bears the same relationship to the ocean that it originally had. Today it is open to the public on a regularly-scheduled basis during spring, summer and fall. Its exhibits of Life-Saving Service equipment include a restored surf-boat, a complete set of beach apparatus with breeches buoy, and several types of line throwing devices.

Cape Cod National Seashore's primary visitor reception facility is the Salt Pond Visitor Center in Eastham. Its exhibits include the individual parts of the beach apparatus—from Lyle gun to breeches bouy—encased for close-up study. Both at this location and at Province Lands Visitor Center in Provincetown, the National Park Service regularly schedules audiovisual presentations about shipwrecks and sea rescue on Cape Cod.

The Highland House Museum, operated by the Truro Historical Society in cooperation with the National Park Service, contains additional examples of lifesaving equipment as well as remnants of shipwrecks; notably items that washed ashore in Truro from the 1898 wreck of the passenger steamer *Portland*.

Besides Old Harbor Station, one other Cape Cod Life-Saving Station has survived. The Cahoon's Hollow Station in Wellfleet remains on its original site. Despite architectural modifications, it is still readily recognizable. As of 1991, it houses a nightclub.

A "half-way house" (pictured and described on page 35) from Cape Cod is in the collection of Mystic Seaport in Connecticut. Mystic Seaport also has a Life-Saving Station, from Block Island. It is an earlier type than the ones that were constructed on Cape Cod and resembles the illustration on page 25 of this book.

Other than these objects and structures, a few foundations—and, in one case, a beach—apparatus drill pole—remain as tangible reminders of Cape Cod's Life-Saving Stations in the closing years of the 20th Century.

******

The Life-Saving Service provided the first major, lasting US Government presence on Cape Cod. The book you are about to read describes the stations and men of the Life-Saving Service at the high point of their place in history. J. W. Dalton's first-person account is a rare gem in its detail and accuracy. We are fortunate that such an observant recorder was on hand to preserve this information.

G. Franklin Ackerman
Chief, Interpretation & Cultural Resources Management
Cape Cod National Seashore
South Wellfleet, Massachusetts
March, 1991

*To my friend George Rounce
with my Best Wishes
Ed Walker
10 Oct 1991*

© Copyright 1902 by J. W. Dalton

Reprinted 1967 by Chatham Press

This edition Published by

PARNASSUS IMPRINTS

Orleans, Massachusetts
May, 1991

ISBN 0-940160-49-8

GOING OFF TO A WRECK.

THE
LIFE SAVERS
OF
CAPE COD

BY

J. W. DALTON
Sandwich, Massachusetts

The Life Savers of Cape Cod.

SURFMAN WALKER, ORLEANS STATION, DRESSED FOR STORMY NIGHT ON THE BEACH.

Cape Cod's life savers are known the world over for their intrepid, enduring bravery, gallant deeds, and the success in rescuing life that they have achieved in their hazardous duties along the most dangerous winter coast of the world.

Every night, along the shores of Cape Cod, from Wood End at Provincetown to Monomoy at Chatham, in moonlight, starlight, thick darkness, driving tempest, wind, rain, snow or hail, an endless line of life savers steadily march along the exposed beaches on the outlook for endangered vessels.

The life saver's work is always arduous, often terrible. Quicksands, the blinding snow and cutting sand storms, the fearful blasts of winter gales, are more often than not to be encountered on their journeys; storm tides, flooding the beaches, drive them to the tops or back of the sand dunes, where they plod along their solitary patrol with great peril.

When a ship is in distress, whatever way the crew is rescued by the life savers, the task involves great hazard of their lives, hours of racking labor, protracted exposure to the roughest weather conditions, and a mental and bodily strain under the spur of exigency and the curb of discipline that exhaust even these hardy fearless coast guardians. In cases of boat service tremendous additional peril and hardships are added.

Death has often claimed the life saver at his work. Or as a result of his gallant, unselfish toil for the safety of others in the rigors of winter, one life saver after another is compelled to retire from the service on account of shattered health.

Beyond their wages of sixty-five dollars per month the surfmen

MAP OF CAPE COD, SHOWING LOCATION OF U. S. L. S. STATIONS.
Small circles show where principal wrecks have taken place within past fifty years.

receive no allowances or emoluments of any kind except the quarters and fuel provided at the stations.

No person belonging to the service is allowed to hold an interest in or to be connected with any wrecking company, nor is he entitled

The Life Savers of Cape Cod. 7

to salvage upon any property he may save or assist to save. A surfman cannot be discharged from the service without good and sufficient reason. For well proven neglect of patrol duty or for disobedience or insubordination at a wreck the keeper may instantly discharge him; in all other cases special authority must be first obtained from the general superintendent.

The keeper lives at his station throughout the year, thus being on hand during the two summer months to summon the crew and volunteers in case of shipwreck or accident.

In "The Life Savers of Cape Cod" it has been the aim of the author to pen-picture some of the heroic deeds performed by these guardians of the "ocean graveyard," as the shores of Cape Cod are known, the terrible hardships they are called upon to endure, and the peril they constantly face in the work of saving life and property, together with illustrations of the life-saving stations on Cape Cod, the boats, beach apparatus, breeches-buoy, etc., used in saving lives, photographs of the crews of the different stations, a historical sketch of the life-saving service, and stories of historic disasters, with biographies of the life savers of Cape Cod, their duties, manner of living, and their achievements.

Cape Cod extends directly out into the Atlantic, like a gigantic arm with clutched hand, bidding defiance to the mighty ocean, for a distance of forty miles. Shifting sand bars parallel its eastern shores, which are an unbroken line of sandy beaches from Monomoy Point at Chatham to Wood End at Provincetown, a distance of about fifty miles. Myriads of shoals lie along the coast, and unnumbered vessels have met their doom along its shores, which rightly bear the name "Ocean Graveyard."

The shores of Cape Cod from Monomoy to Wood End are literally strewn with the bones of once staunch crafts, while unmarked graves in the burial-places in the villages along the coast mutely relate the sad tale of the sacrifice of human life.

Scenes of awful terror and heroic rescues have taken place at the time of shipwreck along these shifting sand bars, and here, too, the life savers have given up their lives in devotion to their duty.

HISTORIC WRECKS.

Thousands of lives have been lost in the wrecks that have taken place along the shores of Cape Cod since the *Mayflower* cast anchor in the harbor at Provincetown in 1620. There is no record of the disasters previous to the establishment of the United States Life-Saving Service in 1872, other than mention in town records and histories of the dates and circumstances of the most memorable, or those attended by great loss of life.

The first shipwreck on Cape Cod, of which there is any record, occurred in 1626, when the historic ship *Sparrowhawk*, Captain Johnson, from England, with colonists bound for Virginia, stranded on

BRITISH FRIGATE SOMERSET.

the shoals near Orleans, and became a total loss. The story of the wreck is told by Governor Bradford in his diary of the Plymouth Colony. The ship's bones were discovered in a mud bank in 1863, the washing away of the shore line disclosing them to view.

Another historic wreck was that of the British frigate *Somerset*, which stranded on Peaked Hill Bars, Nov. 2 or 3, 1778. The *Somerset* was one of the fleet of British men-of-war, whose guns had stormed the heights of Bunker Hill, and terrorized the commerce of

AN OLD WRECK.

the colonies. She was at anchor in Boston Harbor the night that Paul Revere made his famous ride. When she met with disaster she was in pursuit of a fleet of French ships, which were reported to be in Boston Harbor. The *Somerset* had been at anchor in Provincetown harbor for some time, leaving there a few days before she was lost, to go in search of the French ships. She struck Peaked Hill Bars during a northeast gale, while trying to round the Cape, and enter the harbor at Provincetown. She had a complement of four hundred and eighty men, and is supposed to have carried sixty guns, thirty-two, twenty-four, and twelve pounders. She struck on the bars with terrific force, and instantly the seas began to pound her to pieces.

MATILDA BUCK.

She was finally thrown up on the beach by the tumultuous walls of water, and Captain Aurey and the few of the crew who had not perished reached the shore.

The residents of Provincetown viewed the wreck from High Pole Hill, and summoned Capt. Enoch Hallett, of Yarmouth, and Colonel Doane, of Wellfleet, who, with a detachment of militia, made Captain Aurey and the survivors prisoners.

Captain Hallett took charge of the prisoners, marching them up the Cape to Barnstable, and later to Boston, Colonel Doane being left to look after the wrecked craft. There was much jubilation on Cape Cod and in Boston over the disaster. The bones of the *Somerset* remained buried for a century, when the shifting sands exposed them to view. Relic hunters soon carried away nearly all of the wreckage that could be obtained, and the shifting sands have again entombed what remains of the famous old frigate.

Another historic wreck was that of the pirate ship *Widdah*, which was lost near the site of the Cahoon's Hollow Life-Saving Station in 1718. The ship was commanded by Captain Bellamy, and carried twenty-three guns and a crew of one hundred and thirty men. Captain Bellamy had captured seven vessels off the shores of Cape Cod, and on one of them had placed seven of his crew. The captain of the captured ship ran his vessel close to the shore, and the seven pirates were taken prisoners. Later six of them were executed in Boston.

A BAD WRECK.

The *Widdah* soon after was driven ashore during a gale, and all hands, save an Englishman and an Indian, were lost.

A scene of awful terror occurred when the *Josephus*, a British ship, was wrecked on Peaked Hill Bars in the year 1842. She had a cargo of iron rails. Her crew had been driven to the rigging as soon as the vessel struck, and one after another they were seen to fall into the raging sea. Those who had gathered on the shore could hear the despairing cries of the imperiled crew, but were powerless to aid them. At last two of the spectators, Daniel Cassidy and Jonathan Collins, procured a dory, and against the earnest pleadings of their friends, and in the almost certain assurance that they were going to their death, pushed off from the beach, saying as a last farewell, "We can't stand this any longer; we are going to try and rescue those poor fellows if it cost us our lives." Half-way out to the wreck the two heroes successfully battled with the sea, then a giant comber, catching their frail boat, carried it along and buried it under tons of tumbling water. The gallant men were seen to rise and struggle desperately to reach the overturned boat, but perished in the attempt.

WRECKERS AT WORK ON KATIE J. BARRETT.

The men remaining in the rigging of the *Josephus* were soon after swept to death by the monstrous waves that tore the ship to pieces.

In 1848 the brig *Cactus* was lost on the bars along the back of the Cape.

Along the shore near the Cahoon's Hollow Station the immigrant ship *Franklin* was deliberately run ashore in 1849, and many of her poor, helpless passengers perished in the disaster. This was one of the most appalling disasters that ever occurred on Cape Cod. Speedy retribution came to the officers of the ship for their terrible crime, the captain and nearly all the others losing their own lives in the wreck. The late Capt. Benjamin S. Rich, afterwards of the United States Life-Saving Service, was the first to discover the wreck, and also found a box containing some papers that subsequently proved that the disaster was intentional.

The year 1853 was a memorable one in the history of Cape Cod, there being twenty-three appalling disasters along its shore during that period. Among the vessels lost were many ships and brigs well known in shipping circles in Boston and on Cape Cod. The weather

KATIE J. BARRETT BREAKING UP.

was bitter cold and violent storms swept the coast when most of the vessels were lost, so that nothing could be done to assist the imperiled crews, and those who did reach the shore perished from exposure on the desolate uplands and beaches.

In 1866 the *White Squall*, built for a blockade runner, while on her way home from China, struck on the bars along the back of the Cape and became a total loss.

The wreck of the *Aurora* is known to Cape Codders as the "Palm Oil Wreck." The vessel was loaded with palm oil from the west coast of Africa. She struck on the bars off the back of the Cape, and was a total loss.

Another terrible disaster was the wreck of the schooner *Clara Belle*, coal laden, which stranded on the bars off High Head Station, on the night of March 6, 1872, at the height of a fearful blizzard. Captain Amesbury and crew of six men attempted to reach the shore in their boat. The craft had gone but a few yards when she was overturned, throwing the men into the sea. John Silva was the only member of the crew that reached the shore. He found himself alone on a frozen beach with the mercury below zero. He wandered about during the night trying to find some place of shelter, and was found the next morning by a farmer standing dazed, barefooted, and helpless in the highway three miles from the scene of the wreck. His feet and hands were frozen, and it was a long time before he recovered from the

KATIE J. BARRETT JUST BEFORE HER FOREMAST FELL.

effects. The schooner was driven high and dry on the beach, and when boarded the next day a warm fire was found in the cabin. The haste of the crew to leave the vessel had cost them their lives.

The first fearful disaster after the life-saving service re-organization, took place on Peaked Hill Bars, March 4, 1875, when the Italian bark *Giovanni* became a total loss and her crew of fourteen perished. The bark stranded too far from the beach to be reached by the wreck ordnance used in those days, and the surf was pounding on the shore with such fury that a boat could not be launched, much less live, in the sea. No assistance could be rendered the poor sailors, and one by one they dropped into the sea and were lost.

The most appalling disaster in the history of the life-saving service on Cape Cod was the wreck of the iron ship *Jason*, on the bars at Pamet River, Dec. 5, 1893. Twenty-four lives were lost. The ship was bound from Calcutta, India, for Boston, with a cargo of jute. Captain McMillan, who was in charge of the ship, had a crew of twenty-four men, including an apprentice, Samuel J. Evans, of Raglan, England. Thick weather prevailed off the coast for several days preceding the disaster, and Captain McMillan, not being in possession of reliable information as to his position, obtained it from a New York pilot boat.

When about one hundred miles off the coast he unfortunately shaped his course to the westward for the purpose of raising some

AT THE MERCY OF THE SEA.

landmark. When the *Jason* approached the Cape, the wind was blowing a gale from the northeast, and the atmosphere was thick with rain, which soon turned to sleet and snow.

The life savers along the shore at Nauset first saw the *Jason*, and word that a ship was in dangerous proximity to the shore was sent along the Cape to all the stations. The *Jason* was last seen just before five o'clock by the day patrol of the Nauset Station. The life savers, knowing that she could hardly weather the Cape, kept a sharp lookout for her, and at all the stations the horses were hitched into the beach carts and every preparation made to go to the assistance of the ship without a moment's delay. It was a fearful night along the shores of Cape Cod, the coast guardians having all they could do to go over their patrol. Nothing was seen or heard of the doomed ship up to seven o'clock in the evening, and the life savers hoped that she had managed to work offshore or around the Cape. At half-past seven, however, Surfman Honey, of the Pamet River Station, burst into the station, and shouted, "Hopkins (the north patrol) has just burned his signal." A moment later Hopkins rushed into the station and reported that the *Jason* had struck on the bars about a half mile north of the station. Keeper Rich and his crew were ready for the emergency, and, with the beach cart, rushed to the scene. The shore was then piled with wreckage, and the slatting of the sails of the wrecked ship sounded above the roar and din of the storm. A careful lookout for the shipwrecked seafarers was kept by the life savers as

SHIP JASON THE MORNING AFTER SHE WAS WRECKED.

they hurried to the scene, and Evans, the sole survivor of the disaster, was found clinging to a bale of jute. He was clad only in his underclothes, and was almost totally helpless.

The wrecked vessel was sighted through the storm and a shot promptly fired over the craft, but the crew had perished almost as soon as the ship struck, and the efforts of the life savers were of no avail. The ship (it was afterwards learned from young Evans) broke in two almost as soon as she struck, and the members of the crew perished shortly after. Evans told the author that as soon as the ship struck he put on a life-preserver and took to the rigging. The captain ordered the boats launched, but they were smashed as soon as they struck the water. While clinging to the rigging, considering what was best to do, Evans says that he must have been hit by a big wave or wall of water, as the next that he knew he was on the beach and the life savers were taking him to the station. The bodies of twenty of the crew were found and buried in the cemetery at Wellfleet. Evans soon recovered from the effects of the buffeting he received by the seas, and returned to his home in England. Part of

SAMUEL J. EVANS, SOLE SURVIVOR OF WRECKED SHIP JASON,
With life preserver which he wore when cast ashore.

the ship is now visible at low tide, and is an object of much interest to visitors to Cape Cod.

The wreck of the ship *Asia*, in which twenty lives were lost, occurred on Nantucket shoals, near the Great Round Shoal Lightship in February, 1898. The ship was on her way from Manila for Boston, and was commanded by Captain Dakin. Besides the crew of twenty-three men Captain Dakin's wife and little daughter were aboard.

The ship struck on the shoals during a furious northeast gale and snowstorm on Sunday afternoon, but did not begin to break up until the next day.

When the ship commenced to pound to pieces, the mate and the few members of the crew who had not been swept overboard did all in their power to assist Captain Dakin in shielding his wife and daughter from being swept away by the seas which were breaking over the craft. Before the ship broke up, the mate lashed the captain's daughter and himself to a big piece of wreckage, hoping in that way to reach the shore. Captain Dakin and his wife were swept to death before they could fasten themselves to any of the wreckage. Of the whole number aboard the ill-fated craft but three were saved. These were

SHIP ASIA WRECKED ON GREAT ROUND SHOAL.

sailors, who clung to a piece of the ship, and after drifting about in Vineyard Sound for several days, were picked up nearly dead and placed aboard one of the lightships. The bodies of the mate, with his arms locked about the captain's daughter, and both securely lashed to a piece of wreckage, were picked up a few days later in Vineyard Sound. Both had been frozen to death. But few of the bodies of the other members of the crew were found. The ship became a total loss, and the following day there was not a vestige of her left to mark the spot where the tragedy took place.

The schooner *Job H. Jackson* was another terrible wreck that occurred on Peaked Hill Bars. The schooner struck on Jan. 5, 1895, during bitter cold weather, and the crew were driven into the rigging. A fearful sea was pounding on the shore, and it required the combined herculean efforts of the Peaked Hill Bars, Race Point, and High Head life-saving crews, with their life-boats, to rescue the imperiled seafarers, who were badly frost-bitten and helpless when taken from the wrecked vessel.

The schooner *Daniel B. Fearing*, which became a total loss on the bars off Cahoon's Hollow Station, struck there during a fog on May 6, 1896. The life savers put off to the wreck in their surfboat, and brought the crew ashore. A gale sprung up with great suddenness as the crew were leaving the doomed vessel, and as the last man

JOHN S. PARKER, WHICH BECAME A TOTAL LOSS ON NAUSET BARS.

jumped into the life-boat the masts of the big schooner fell with a crash, and the sea soon completed the work of total destruction.

On Sept. 14, 1896, the Italian bark *Monte Tabor* struck on Peaked Hill Bars during a furious northeast gale. The disaster was attended with the loss of five men, whose deaths were involved in circumstances of mysterious and almost romantic interest. Three were suicides, while the manner in which the other two perished could not be certainly explained. The bark hailed from Genoa, and carried a crew of twelve persons, including the officers and two boys. She had a cargo of salt from Trapani, Island of Sicily, for Boston. The craft had been struck by a hurricane on September 9, and when off Cape Cod on the night of the 13th, in endeavoring to make the harbor at Provincetown,

A TOTAL WRECK.

she struck the dreaded Peaked Hill Bars. She was discovered by Patrolman Silvey, of the Peaked Hill Bars Station. The night was pitch dark, the surf extremely high, and the bark was soon pounded to pieces. As the life-saving crews could not locate the wreck, there was

STRUCK WITH ALL SAILS SET.

nothing to shoot at and nothing to pull to, even if a boat could have been launched. It is believed that the captain was so humiliated by the loss of his vessel, that he fell into a frenzy of despair, and resolved to take his own life, and it would appear that others of his crew followed his example of self-destruction.

Six of the crew managed to reach the shore on the top of the cabin, and were pulled out of the surf by the life savers. Another, a boy, said that he swam ashore. An investigation, conducted by the Italian counsel, disclosed that the captain committed suicide.

The first evidence that the steamer *Portland* had met with disaster during the memorable gale of November, 1898, was found by John

WRECKAGE WHICH CAME ASHORE AFTER THE STEAMER PORTLAND WAS LOST AND LIFE PRESERVER FROM THE ILL-FATED CRAFT.

Life preserver in right foreground.

Johnson, a surfman of the Race Point Station, who picked up a life-preserver from the ill-fated craft.

Soon after Johnson found the life-preserver, wreckage from the steamer was seen in the surf along the shore, and within a short time the beach for miles was strewn with it. All the life savers suffered great hardship during that gale, which was the worst in the history of the life-saving service.

Twice since the establishment of the United States Life-Saving Service on Cape Cod, the life savers in the life-boats have met with disaster, and members of the crews perished in the catastrophe.

The Life Savers of Cape Cod.

CHARLES A. CAMPBELL WRECKED AT PAMET RIVER.

Keeper David H. Atkins and Surfman Frank Mayo and Elisha Taylor of the Peaked Hill Bars Station perished by their boat being wrecked during a second trip to the stone-loaded sloop, *C. E. Trum-*

LILLIE ABANDONED AND IN A BAD PLACE.

bull, on the morning of Nov. 30, 1880, to take off two sailors who refused to go ashore the first time.

Surfman S. O. Fisher, now keeper of the Race Point Station, C. P. Kelley, now keeper at High Head Station, and Isaiah Young, who has not since seen a well day, lived to tell the story after a life or death struggle with icy seas and currents and being swept for miles along the shore before they crawled up on the beach.

But the Monomoy disaster of March 17, 1902 was the most appalling and attended with the greatest loss of life, twelve men, seven of them life savers, perishing.

The conduct of the Monomoy crew on this occasion affords a note-

SCHOONER BEING POUNDED TO PIECES OFF ORLEANS.

worthy example of unflinching fidelity to duty. By long experience they were fully aware of the perils that must be encountered in going to the wrecked vessels, but it was a summons which the brave and conscientious life savers could not disregard.

The story of this disaster is still fresh in the public mind.

THE ESTABLISHMENT OF THE LIFE-SAVING SERVICE ON CAPE COD.

The establishment of the United States Life-Saving Service on Cape Cod dates back but thirty years, which time also marks the reorganization, extension, and beginning of its efficiency in the United States. While as early as 1797 the town of Truro sold to the United States

Government a tract of land upon which to erect the first lighthouse on Cape Cod, — Highland Light, so called, — it was not until half a century later that the government began to provide means for the relief of mariners wrecked upon its coasts, and seventy-five years afterwards that the first United States Life-Saving Station was erected on the shores of Cape Cod.

The Massachusetts Humane Society, originally formed in 1786, and incorporated for general purposes of benevolence a few years later, was the first to attempt organized relief for shipwrecked seafarers in the United States as well as upon Cape Cod.

The Society first began its work of rendering assistance to ship-

ONE OF THE FIRST LIFE-SAVING CREWS.

wrecked mariners by building huts on many of the desolate sections of the coast. These huts were for the shelter of shipwrecked persons who might reach the shore. The first building of this kind was erected on Lovell's Island in Boston Harbor in 1807. Later, the Society established the first life-boat station at Cohasset, subsequently erecting others along the coast, and extending its good work to the shores of Cape Cod.

While the Society relied solely upon volunteer crews to man these life-boats in times of disaster, its efforts in saving life and property were of great value, and both the state and general government tendered it pecuniary aid at various times. When the government extended the life-saving service to Cape Cod, the Society was relieved of its burden of protecting that dangerous coast, thus enabling it to better provide for other sections of the coast of Massachusetts.

The Massachusetts Humane Society may be considered the parent of the United States Life-Saving Service. The Society is one of the oldest in the world. It originated its coast service more than thirty-six years before the English did, while the French service dates its birth much later.

In 1845, a few years before Congress took steps for providing means for rendering assistance to wrecked vessels along the coasts of the United States, the Society had eighteen stations on the Massachusetts coast, with boats and mortars for throwing life lines to stranded vessels, in addition to numerous huts of refuge.

ETHEL MAUD BEING BURIED IN THE SAND.

With the exception of the Life-Saving Benevolent Association of New York, chartered by the Legislature of that State in 1849, no other successful organized efforts outside of those of the government were made up to this time to lessen the distress incident to shipwreck.

The first appropriation made by Congress for rendering assistance to the shipwrecked from shore was March 3, 1847. For nearly a half century prior to this time the efforts of the government for the protection of mariners upon the coasts of the United States were mainly in establishing the coast survey and extending the lighthouse system.

In 1848 the attention of Congress was called to the immediate needs of providing further means for rendering assistance to wrecked vessels along the Atlantic coast, and a second appropriation of $10,000 was made. The first appropriation of $5,000 remained in the treasury as an unexpended balance.

Later, this money was placed in the hands of the Collector of Customs at Boston for the benefit of the Massachusetts Humane Society, for use in the work of building and equipping new life stations along the Massachusetts coast.

The second appropriation of $10,000 was for expenditure upon the New Jersey coast. With this appropriation eight boat-houses were erected and supplied with appliances for saving life and property. This marks the beginning of the life-saving service of the United States.

In 1849 Congress appropriated $20,000 for life-saving purposes. With this sum eight life-saving stations were built on the Long Island coast and six additional stations erected on the shores of New Jersey. While these newly established life-saving stations were not manned by regular drilled crews of surfmen, as at present, they often proved of great

ONE OF THE FIRST UNITED STATES LIFE-SAVING STATIONS.

value at times of disaster, and in 1850 Congress made another appropriation of $20,000 for life-saving purposes.

Of this sum half was expended in erecting additional stations along the shores of Long Island, and for a new station at Watch Hill, R. I.

The attention of Congress having been called to the needs of some means of rendering assistance to wrecked vessels along the coasts of North and South Carolina, Georgia, Florida, and Texas, the remaining $10,000 of this appropriation was expended in placing lifeboats at the most exposed points on these coasts.

In 1853 and 1854 Congress made liberal appropriations for lifesaving purposes, and fourteen new stations were built on the coast of New Jersey.

The service was at this time extended to the Great Lakes, twenty-three life-boats being stationed at different points on Lake Michigan, and several others on the other lake shores and on the Atlantic coast. In 1854 there were one hundred and thirty-seven life-boats stationed along the coasts of the United States. Of this number fifty-five were at stations on the New York and New Jersey coasts.

HAROLDINE STRANDED ON NAUSET BARS.

The absence of drilled and disciplined crews at these stations, however, — together with irresponsible custodians and the lack of proper equipments, the result of pillage or decay, — contributed to great loss of life and heartrending scenes of disaster along the Atlantic coast. The inefficiency of the life-saving service, as it then existed, was apparent to all. Public sentiment had now become excited, and Con-

AFTER THE BEACH COMBERS HAVE WORKED ON THE WRECK.

gress was appealed to for immediate relief from the existing conditions.

In 1853 a bill which provided for the increase and repair of the stations and the guardianship of the life-boats passed the Senate; but, unfortunately, failed to reach the House before adjournment. An appalling disaster, the wreck of the *Powhatan*, on the coast of New Jersey, in which three hundred lives were lost, caused the bill to be promptly and favorably acted upon at the next session of Congress. Under the provisions of this bill a superintendent at a salary of $1,500 per annum was appointed for the Atlantic and Lake coasts, keepers were placed in charge of the stations at a salary of $200,

ELSIE M. SMITH, WHICH BECAME A TOTAL LOSS ON NAUSET BEACH.

bonded custodians secured for the life-boats and other apparatus, and the stations and equipments speedily put in order.

The service was somewhat improved as a result of this, but there were still many defects in it, which were brought to light as disaster followed disaster along the seaboard. Up to this time the life-saving crews were not regularly employed.

A bill providing for the employment of regular crews of surfmen was presented to Congress in 1869. Strange though it may seem, in view of the terrible disasters and loss of life which had so recently taken place along the Atlantic coast, the bill suffered defeat. A substitute bill, however, which provided for the employment of crews of surfmen, though only at alternate stations, was passed. This marks

SHIP A. S. ROPES DISMASTED OFF PROVINCETOWN DURING A GALE.

the beginning of the employment of crews of surfmen at the United States life-saving stations, and was the first step in the direction of their employment at all stations for regular periods.

During the winter of 1870–71 a number of appalling, fatal disasters occurred along the Atlantic coast. These disasters not only revealed the fact that the coast was not properly guarded, but also that the service was inefficient and needed a more complete organization. In 1871 Congress again appropriated $200,000 and authorized the Secretary of the Treasury to employ crews of surfmen at such stations and for such periods as he might deem necessary.

Mr. Sumner I. Kimball, the present general superintendent of the United States Life-Saving Service, was at that time in charge of the Revenue Marine Service, and the life-saving stations being then under the charge of that bureau, he at once took steps to ascertain the conditions of the service.

An officer of the Revenue Marine Service was at once detailed to visit the life-saving stations and to make a report of their condition and requirements.

The report made by the officer was a startling revelation. Absolutely no discipline was found among the crews, no care had been taken of the apparatus, some of the stations were in ruins, others lacked such articles as powder, rockets, and shot lines, every portable article had been stolen from many stations, and the money that Congress had appropriated had been practically wasted.

From the report it was plainly evident that the reorganization of the service must be speedily brought about, and in accordance with an act of Congress in 1872, the organization of the present system of life-saving districts with superintendents took place.

The inefficient keepers were at once removed and the most skilled boatmen obtainable were placed in charge of the stations.

The stations were also manned by the most expert surfmen to be found along the coast, and the patrol of the coast at night and during thick weather by day was inaugurated. It was soon found that the life-saving stations, however, were too far apart for the crews to be of assistance to one another in the event of a wreck, and measures were adopted to place them within distances of from three to five miles of one another. To bring about this result, twelve new stations were built on the New Jersey coast, six on Long Island, while the location of some of the existing stations were changed.

The stations were plain houses forty-two feet long and eighteen wide, of two stories and four rooms. One room below was used by the crew as mess-room, the other room contained the boats and other apparatus used at wrecks. One of the upper rooms was used as a sleeping room for the crew, the other room was used as a storeroom.

As a result of the reorganization of the service, the record for the first season shows that not a life was lost in the disasters that occurred on either the Lake shores or the Atlantic coast.

Interest in the success of the life-saving service under the new

AN ABANDONED FISHERMAN IN A BAD PLACE.

system was now keyed up to a high pitch. Congress had authorized a new station for the coast of Rhode Island in 1871, and in June, 1872, one more was ordered for that coast, and nine for the coast of Cape Cod. These stations were built and manned in the winter of 1872. The nine that were erected on Cape Cod were located as follows: Race Point and Peaked Hill Bars, at Provincetown; Highlands, at North Truro; Pamet River, at Truro; Cahoon's Hollow, at Wellfleet; Nauset, at North Eastham; Orleans, at Orleans; Chatham, at Chatham; and Monomoy, on Monomoy Island. Since that time four new

THE LIFE-SAVERS MESS ROOM, NAUSET STATION.

stations have been established, the Wood End, High Head, Old Harbor, and Monomoy Point.

The life-saving stations on Cape Cod are situated among the sand hills common to the eastern shores of the Cape, at distances back from the high-water mark as to insure their safety. In most instances they are plain structures, designed to serve as a home for the crew and to afford storage for the boats and other apparatus. In most of the stations on Cape Cod the lower floor is divided into five rooms — a mess room, which also serves for a sitting room for the crew, a kitchen, a keeper's room, a boat and beach apparatus room. Wide double-leafed doors with a sloping platform permit the quick and easy running out of the surf-boat and other apparatus from the station.

The second story contains two rooms: one the sleeping room for the crew; the other has spare cots for rescued persons, and is also used as a storeroom.

On every station there is a lookout or observatory, from which the life savers, during the day when the weather is fair, keep a careful watch of all shipping along the coast. In order that the life-saving stations may be distinguished from a long distance at sea, they are usually painted dark red, and as a further aid to shipping, they are marked by a flagstaff about sixty feet high erected close by them. This flagstaff is also used to signal passing vessels by the International code. These stations are manned from the 1st of August until June

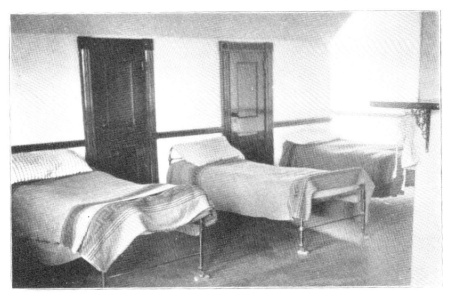

THE SIMPLY FURNISHED SLEEPING QUARTERS, CAHOON'S HOLLOW STATION.

1st following, the keeper remaining on duty throughout the year. The stations are generally furnished with two surf-boats (supplied with oars, life preservers, life-boat compass, drag, boat-hooks, hatchet, heaving line, knife, bucket, and other outfits), boat carriages, two sets of breeches-buoy apparatus (including guns and accessories), carts for the transportation of the apparatus, a life-car, cork-jackets (life preservers), Coston signals, signal rockets, signal flags of the International and General signal code, medicine chests with contents, patrol lanterns, barometer, thermometer, patrol clocks, the requisite furniture for housekeeping by the crew and for the succor of rescued persons, fuel, oil, tools for the repair of the boats and apparatus, and minor repairs to the buildings, and the necessary books and stationery.

With the International and General code of signals, shipping, when miles at sea, can, by this means, open communication with the stations, be reported, obtain latitude and longtitude, or, if disabled, can thus send for assistance.

All the life-saving stations on Cape Cod are connected by telephone with lines running to central stations in Provincetown and Chatham. Close watch of the movements of all shipping is in this way easily maintained, and in time of disaster help is quickly summoned and obtained from one station to another.

In the life-saving service the week begins on Sunday night at

BARK KATE HARDING HIGH AND DRY ON THE BEACH AND SOON A TOTAL WRECK.

midnight, and the days are each set apart for some particular kind of employment.

On Monday the members of the crew are employed putting the station in order. On Tuesday, weather permitting, the crew are drilled in launching and landing in the life-boat through the surf.

On Wednesday the men are drilled in the International and General code of signals.

Thursday, the crew drill with the beach apparatus and breeches-buoy.

Friday, the crew practice the resuscitation drill for restoring the apparently drowned.

Saturday is wash-day.

Sunday is devoted to religious practices.

The Life Savers of Cape Cod. 33

SALARIES OF THE KEEPERS AND SURFMEN.

The keepers of the life-saving stations receive $900 per year for their services, and the surfmen $65 per month.

In the early history of the life-saving service the keepers received but $200 per year, later their salary was increased to $400, then to $700, and, finally, to the present figure.

The surfmen in the early days of the service received but $40 per month, later it was increased to $45, then to $60, and, finally, to the present sum.

At the opening of the "active season," August 1 of each year, the

BEACH COMBERS AT WORK STRIPPING THE WRECKED FISHING VESSEL FORTUNA.

men assemble at their respective stations and establish themselves for a residence of ten months, being allowed one day in seven to visit their homes between sunrise and sunset. They arrange for their housekeeping, usually forming a mess, each man taking turns by the week in cooking. The crew is organized by the keeper arranging and numbering them in their supposed order of merit, the most competent and trustworthy being designated as No. 1, the next No. 2, and so on. These numbers are changed by promotion as vacancies occur, or by such rearrangement from time to time as proficiency in drill and performance of duty may dictate. Whenever the keeper is absent, the No. 1 surfman assumes command and exercises the keeper's functions. When the rank of the crew has been fixed, the keeper assigns to each his position and prepares station bills for the day watch, night patrol, boat and apparatus drill, care of the station, etc. Then all is ready for the active work and the watch of the sea and shore that never ceases, day or night, until the close of the active season ten months later.

The patrol of the beaches each night, and during thick weather by day, by which stranded vessels are promptly discovered and the rescue of the imperiled crews made the object of effort by the life saver, distinguishes the United States Life-Saving Service from all others in the world, and in a great measure accounts for its unparalleled triumphs in rescuing shipwrecked seafarers.

If the surfman sights a vessel in distress or running into danger during the night, he fires a brilliant red Coston signal which he always carries. This is a signal to the shipwrecked crew that they have been seen and assistance has been summoned, and to the crew of a vessel which is approaching the danger line along the coast that it is time to haul offshore.

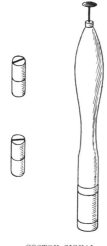

COSTON SIGNAL.

During the daylight on clear days the watch is kept from a lookout on the station, or by observation from points where the entire beach and sea limits of the station's district can be clearly seen. Foggy days, and during thick weather, and every night, fair or foul, the watch is by the patrol of every foot of the water front of each district. The stations are located about five miles apart, and the district patrol beats of each are thus about two and one-half miles on either side of the station. The boundaries of each district are marked by a little hut in some protected spot on the beach called "The half-way house," except at the Wood End Station. The night patrol is divided into four watches, one from sunset to 8 o'clock (the dog watch), one from 8 to 12, one from 12 to 4, and one from 4 to sunrise. Two surfmen are designated for each watch.

When the time for their patrol arrives, the surfmen set out from the station, in opposite directions, keeping well down on the beach as near the surf as possible until they reach the half-way house. Here they get warmed, and the surfmen from the adjoining station are met and checks exchanged. If a patrolman fails to meet the patrolman from the adjoining station at the half-way house, he, after waiting for a reasonable time, continues his journey until he either meets the patrolman or reaches the other station and ascertains the cause of failure. He thus patrols the neglected shore and is at hand to assist in case of disaster detaining the other patrolman. At the stations where the patrolmen carry watchmen's time-clocks the key is

HALF-WAY HOUSE, WHERE SURFMEN FROM ADJOINING STATIONS MEET AND EXCHANGE CHECKS.

These houses are connected with the stations by telephone, and often from here the keepers are notified of disaster, and the crew summoned to a wreck.

secured to a post at the end of the beat, and the patrolman is required to reach it, wind the clock, and must bring back the dial in his clock properly recorded.

The means employed at the life-saving stations for rescuing persons from wrecked vessels is everywhere essentially the same, either a life-boat is sent out through the surf or the breeches-buoy, or life-car used. The rescues by boat are the most thrilling and hazardous. The method of establishng communication with stranded vessels is over a century old, successful experiments with this method having been made as early as 1791 by Lieutenant Bell of the Royal Artillery. He demonstrated the practicability of the method by means of a mortar, which carried a heavy shot four hundred yards from a vessel to the shore. Lieutenant Bell also observed that a line might be carried from the shore over a stranded vessel by the means of his mortar, but the credit for the actual execution of this method of establishing communication is given to Capt. G. W. Manby, according to a report of a committee of the House of Commons, dated March 10, 1810. A London coach-maker first conceived the idea of a life-boat. The present type is the product of a century's devoted study and experiment.

A SURFMAN'S CHECK.

Practice drills in the use of the breeches-buoy and surf-boats are carried on constantly at each station, until so proficient are the crews that practice rescues are often made in less than three minutes. The practice is carried on under conditions as near active work in a disaster as are possible, and a description of a drill will give the best idea of actual work at a wreck.

For the practice with the beach apparatus, the breeches-buoy, each station has a drill ground prepared by erecting a spar, called a wreck pole, to represent the mast of a stranded vessel seventy-five yards distant. This is over the water, if possible, from the place where the men operate, which represents the shore.

Each man knows in detail every act he is to perform in the exercise from constant practice, and as prescribed in the Service Manual. At

TAKING A MAN ASHORE WITH THE BREECHES-BUOY. LYLE GUN IN FOREGROUND.

the word of command they drag the apparatus to the drill ground, where they effect a mimic rescue by rigging the gear and taking a man ashore from the wreck pole in the breeches-buoy. If one month after the opening of the active season a crew cannot accomplish the rescue within five minutes, it is considered that they have been remiss in drilling.

No such celerity, however, is expected of the life savers in effecting rescues from shipwrecks, when storm, surf, currents, and motion of the stranded crafts conspire to obstruct. The hastening of the work of mimic rescue, however, gives the life-savers the utmost familiarity with the apparatus and prepares them for working speedily and successfully in utter darkness and under the most trying weather conditions.

The boat practice consists in launching and landing through the surf, capsizing and righting the boat, and practice in handling the oars. Drill signaling is interrogating each surfman as to the meaning of the various flags, the use of the code book, and actual conversation carried on by means of sets of miniature signals provided for each station.

The beach apparatus, the breeches-buoy, is used to effect the rescue of shipwrecked seafarers when vessels have stranded near the shore and the conditions make it inexpedient to use the surf-boats. At such

READY FOR A PRACTICE DRILL WITH THE BREECHES-BUOY AND FLAGS.

times the apparatus is hauled to the scene in the beach cart; horses, kept at all the stations for the purpose, assisting the life savers in the work.

Frequently the storms which sweep the beaches are so violent that the horses refuse to pull the cart, and the life savers are then obliged to cover the head of the animals before they can be induced to face the fury of the elements. The life savers when on such journeys are usually driven to the back of the beaches by the tides, and the task of dragging the apparatus over the sand dunes is extremely difficult and hazardous.

The "cut throughs" in the beaches, places where during storms the seas rush through to the lowlands, further contribute to the dangers that confront the life savers as they rush along with the apparatus.

These "cut throughs" are also the dreaded menace of the surfmen on patrol, during stormy weather and high tides, the seas, as they sweep through them, often entrapping the life savers, throwing them down, burying them in the rushing waters, and jeopardizing their lives.

As soon as the life savers reach the scene of disaster, the Lyle gun is quickly taken from the cart, loaded, sighted, and fired, the captain, who sights and fires the gun, taking good care that he has sent the shot flying through the storm well to the windward of the wrecked vessel, so that if the shot should fail to go across the vessel, yet

LIFE SAVERS AND HORSE HARNESSED TO SURF BOAT CART READY TO GO TO A WRECK.

beyond it, the line will be carried to the wreck by the force of the gale.

The work of burying the sand anchor, getting the crotch, whip line, hawser, and breeches-buoy ready is speedily accomplished. Torches are kept burning by the life savers to tell those on the wrecked vessel that assistance is at hand and the life savers are at work, and even if the imperiled crew do not hear the report of the gun, which has fired a shot to the vessel, they at once begin a search for the shot-line which is invariably found somewhere in the rigging.

The captain, with the shore end of the shot-line in his hand, waits for a signal from the ship that the line has passed over the vessel, and

The Life Savers of Cape Cod.

THE BEACH CART, MEN, AND HORSE, WITH HARNESS ON, READY TO GO TO A WRECK.

that the crew have found it and are ready to proceed with the work of rescue. A tail-block with a whip, an endless line rove through it, is made fast to the shot-line, and the wrecked seafarers haul it aboard their vessel as speedily as possible. Attached to the tail-block is a tally board with the following directions in English and French printed on it: —

"Make the tail of the block fast to lower mast well up. If the masts are gone, then to the best place you can find. Cast off shot-line, see that rope in the block runs free, and show signal to shore."

The foregoing instructions having been complied with, the result will be as shown in Figure 1.

As soon as the life savers get a signal from the vessel that the tail-block has been made fast, they "tie"

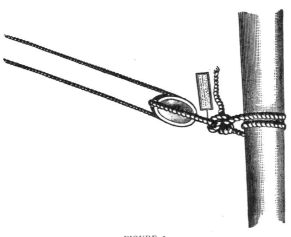

FIGURE I.

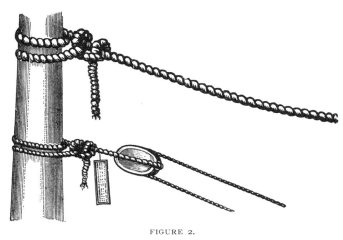

FIGURE 2.

bend on a three-inch hawser to the whip, the endless line, and by it haul the hawser off to the vessel. Occasionally circumstances permit wrecked crews to assist in this part of the work, but usually the life savers are compelled to do it alone. To the end of the hawser, which has been bent on to the whip, the endless line, is also attached a tally board with the following directions in English and French: —

"Make the hawser fast about two feet above the tail-block; see all clear, and that the rope in the block runs free; show signal to the shore."

These instructions being obeyed, the result will be shown as in Figure 2.

Particular care must be taken that there are no turns of the whip, the endless line, around the hawser; to prevent this the end of the hawser is taken up between the parts of the whip, the endless line,

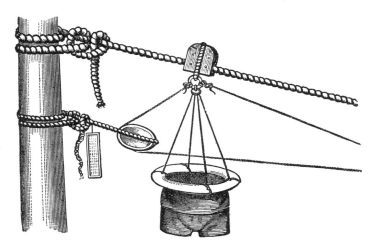

FIGURE 3.

before making it fast. When the hawser is made fast to the wrecked vessel, the whip, the endless line, is cast off from the hawser, and the life savers, having been signaled to this effect, make the shore end of the hawser fast to the strap of the sand anchor. The crotch is then placed under the hawser and raised, and the latter drawn as taut as possible, thus making a slender bridge of rope between the vessel and shore. The traveler block, from which is suspended the breeches-buoy, is then put on the hawser, the whip, the endless line, made fast to breeches-buoy, and thus hauled to and from the vessel, as shown in Figure 3, which represent the apparatus rigged with the breeches-buoy hauled out to the vessel.

SHOT USED WITH LYLE GUN.

The life savers always carry a good supply of shot and lines with them, and if the first shot fails to carry the line to the vessel, which seldom occurs, owing to the skill of those who have charge of this important branch of the work, a second one is promptly fired. The work of hauling the breeches-buoy to and from a wrecked vessel is an arduous task. The whip, the endless line, after passing through the seas, becomes coated with ice and sand, which cuts the mittens and lacerates the hands of the surfmen in a fearful manner at times.

The captain and one of the life savers rush into the surf and take the rescued persons out of the breeches-buoy as soon as it reaches the beach, while the other members of the crew stand ready to again send the breeches-buoy off to the wreck as soon as one rescue has been accomplished. In this way one after another of shipwrecked crews are brought ashore.

Women and children and helpless persons are landed first from wrecked vessels. Children when brought ashore in this way are held in the arms of some elder person or securely lashed to the breeches-

LYLE GUN, SHOWING SHOT PROTRUDING FROM THE MUZZLE.

buoy. The instructions to mariners are to remain by the wreck until assistance arrives, unless the vessel shows signs of immediately breaking up. If not discovered immediately by the patrol, the crews of wrecked vessels are instructed to burn rockets, flare up, or other lights, and if the weather is foggy to fire guns.

Under no circumstances should the crew of wrecked vessels attempt to land through the surf in their own boats, until the last hope of assistance from shore has vanished. Often when comparatively smooth at sea, a dangerous surf is running alongshore, which is not perceptible three or four hundred yards offshore, and the surf when viewed from a vessel never appears so dangerous as it is. Many lives have been unnecessarily lost by crews of stranded vessels being thus deceived and attempting to land in the ship's boats.

After a crew has been rescued the work of recovering the apparatus is quickly accomplished, and every part of it except the shot is invariably recovered, and often even the shot is also saved. This is done by a hawser cutter, which is pulled off to the wreck on the hawser the same as the breeches-buoy, cutting the hawser off close to where it is attached to the wrecked vessel. The life savers then haul the apparatus through the sea to the shore.

The first gun used for throwing a line to stranded ships was of cast iron, and weighed two hundred and eighty-eight pounds, and threw a shot weighing twenty-four pounds, with an extreme range of four hundred and twenty-one yards. This soon gave place to an improved gun, which was of cast iron, with steel lining, mounted on a wooden carriage. This gun weighed two hundred and sixty-six pounds, and carried a twenty-four pound shot four hundred and seventy-three yards. The Lyle gun, which is now used by the life savers of Cape Cod, is a bronze smooth bore gun, weighing but one hundred and eighty-five pounds, and fires a cylindrical line, carrying shot, weighing about eighteen pounds, some six hundred and ninety-five yards. This projectile has a shank protruding from the muzzle of the gun to an eye in which the line is tied — a device which prevents, to a degree, the line from being burned off by the ignited gases in firing. As further protection against this happening, the life savers wet that part of the line liable to become burned. When the gun is fired the weight and inertia of the line cause the projectile to reverse. The shot-line is made of unbleached linen thread very closely and smoothly braided, is waterproof, and has great elasticity, which tends to insure it against breaking. The lines in use vary in thickness according to circumstances. They are of three sizes, designated as number 4, 7, and 9, being respectively $\frac{4}{32}$, $\frac{7}{32}$, or $\frac{9}{32}$ of an inch in diameter. Any charge of powder can be used up to the maximum six ounces.

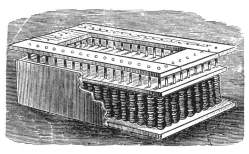

FAKING BOX.

The Lyle gunshot line is

carried in a faking box, so called, a wooden box with handles for convenience for carrying. The line is coiled on wooden pins, layer above layer. When brought into use the pins are withdrawn, and the line lies disposed in layers ready to pay out freely

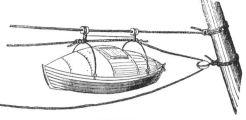

LIFE-CAR.

and fly to the wreck without entanglement. While six hundred and ninety-five yards is the greatest range to be obtained by a Lyle gun, about two hundred yards is considered the working limit. The line sags so, at more than two hundred yards, and the currents are usually so swift, that the crew of a stranded vessel could not haul the whip aboard their craft at a much greater distance, and in addition any one being pulled ashore in the breeches-buoy further than that would most likely perish from the cold and buffeting of the seas before they could be rescued.

The crotch is made of two pieces of wood, three by two inches thick, and ten feet long, securely bolted together, and crossed near the top so as to form a sort of X. The sand anchor is two pieces of hard wood, six feet long, eight inches wide and two inches thick, crossed at their centers, bolted together, and furnished at the center with a stout iron ring. It is laid obliquely in a trench behind the crotch. An iron hook, from which runs a strap of rope, having at its other end an iron ring called bull's-eye, is fastened into the ring of the sand anchor. This strap connects with a double pulley-block at the end of the hawser behind the crotch, by which the hawser is drawn and kept taut. The trench is solidly filled in, and the imbedded sand anchor, held by the lateral strain against the side of the trench, sustains the slender bridge of rope constituted by the hawser between the stranded vessel and the shore.

The large majority of vessels now stranded on the shores of the Cape being coasters, with crews from six to ten men, the breeches-buoy is invariably used in preference to the life-car. It weighs but twenty-one pounds. It consists of a common life-preserver of cork, seven and one-half feet in circumference, to which short canvas breeches are attached. Four rope lanyards, fastened to the circle of this cork, meet above an iron ring, which is attached to a block, called a traveler. The hawser passes through this block, and the suspended breeches-buoy is drawn between ship and shore by a whip, an endless line. At each trip it receives but one person, who gets into it with their legs down through the canvas breeches legs, holding to the lanyards, sustained in a sitting position by the canvas saddle, or seat of the breeches, with his legs dangling below. When there is imminent danger of the vessel breaking up and great haste is required, two persons get into the breeches-buoy at once, and to further expedite the work of rescue, the hawser is dispensed with, part of the hauling line being used for the breeches-buoy to travel on to and from the wreck.

There are many kinds of life-boats, and various devices for effecting communication by line with stranded vessels. The type of boats in use on Cape Cod are the Monomoy and Race Point models. All these boats are distinctly known as surf-boats. They are constructed of cedar with white oak frames, and are from twenty-two to twenty-four feet in length. The surf-boats have air chambers at the ends,

"A PERILOUS TASK." LIFE SAVERS GOING TO A WRECKED VESSEL ON PEAKED HILL BARS.

and are fitted with cork fenders along the outer side to protect them against collisions with hulls or wreckage, and to further aid in keeping them afloat, and righting lines by which they can be righted if capsized in the surf. They weigh from seven hundred to one thousand pounds. In the hands of the skilled surfmen of Cape Cod they are capable of marvelous action, and few sights are more impressive than the surf-boat plowing its way through the breakers, at times riding on top of the surge, at others held in suspension before the roaring tumultuous wall of water, or darting forth as the comber breaks and crumbles, obedient to the oars of the impassive life savers. All these boats are so light that they can be readily transported along the sandy shores of the Cape under normal weather conditions, and launched in very shallow water.

The type of boat that is best suited for one locality, however, may be ill adapted for another, and a boat that would be serviceable at one

HEAVING STICK.

A small line is attached to this, and the life savers find it a very valuable means of getting a line to a vessel or piece of wreckage. It can be used advantageously at about fifty yards.

time might be worse than useless at another. On the coast of Cape Cod the boat service at wrecks is generally not very far off from shore, and the chief and greatest danger lurks in the lines of surf which must be crossed, and in the breakers on the outlying shoals.

The self-righting and bailing boat is more unwieldy, not so quickly responsive to the tactics of the steersman, and not so well adapted to the general work on Cape Cod. Where long excursions are apt to be undertaken, and the service is especially hazardous, the men feel safer in a self-righting and bailing boat, one of which has been introduced at the new Monomoy Point Station.

When the surf-boat is used to effect rescue it is taken along the

WAITING FOR A GOOD CHANCE TO LAUNCH.

LIFE SAVERS PRACTICING LAUNCHING THROUGH THE SURF.

beach to a point as near the wreck as possible, unloaded from the cart, and at a favorable time run into the raging waters. The keeper is the last man to get aboard the surf-boat, climbing in over the stern as she is run into the sea. The life savers who remain ashore to assist in getting the boat off run waist deep into the sea, helping to guide the boat, and to prevent her, if possible, from being capsized in the surf. The keeper steers with a long oar, and with the aid of his trained surfmen, intent upon his every look and command, guides the buoyant craft through the surf with masterly skill. He is usually

A GOOD LAUNCHING. CAPTAIN IN THE ACT OF GETTING INTO THE BOAT.

A GOOD LANDING.

able to avoid a direct encounter with the heaviest breakers, but if he is obliged to let them strike him, he meets them directly "head on."

Although sometimes hurled back upon the beach and broken in desperate and unavailing attempts at a launch against a resistless sea this boat, which might easily be upset, has rarely been capsized in going through the surf. While there is always great peril in launching these boats in times of shipwreck, the greatest danger lies in landing through the surf. The gigantic walls of water speeding to the shore cannot then be met head on as when the boat is passing out,

IN DANGER OF OVERTURNING.

and when one of these tumultuous combers break over the stern of the boat, which, fortunately, has rarely occurred on Cape Cod, the lives of those aboard the craft are placed in great peril.

In landing the life savers jump into the surf as the boat is about to touch the beach, and with the assistance of those of the crew who remained ashore to select a good landing place, the craft is quickly run up on the beach far out of the reach of the dangerous undertow.

This work is also attended with great danger, the surfmen sometimes receiving injuries by being struck by the boat, which incapacitates them from further duty in the service. The keepers and crews

AFTER A WRECK, SURFMEN OF CAHOON'S HOLLOW STATION CARRYING A BODY TO THEIR STATION.

place their faith in the surf-boats which they use, and they are ever ready to face any sea in which a boat will live.

When a distressed vessel is reached, the orders of the keeper, the captain of the crew of life savers, who always steers and commands, must be implicitly obeyed.

There must be no headlong rushing or crowding, and the captain of the ship must remain on board to preserve order until every other person has left. Women, children, and helpless persons are taken into the boat first. Goods or baggage will not be taken into the boat

The Life Savers of Cape Cod.   49

under any circumstances until all persons are landed. If any be passed in against the keeper's remonstrance he throws it overboard.

It often happens, however, that some of the crew, and even captains of wrecked vessels, attempt to get their baggage into the surf-boats. At a wreck which Captain Cole and his crew went to in the night a few years ago the captain of the craft insisted that the life savers should wait until he could get his baggage ready to take ashore. Captain Cole, in a voice that could be heard above the roar and din of the storm, commanded the bow oarsmen, who was holding the painter that kept the surf-boat alongside the wreck, to cut the painter. The captain of the stranded craft no sooner heard this command than he jumped into the boat, leaving his effects behind, and was safely taken ashore.

Persons rescued from shipwreck are taken to the nearest life-saving station, the weak, sick, and the disabled are treated with remedies from the medicine chest, supplied under the direction of the Surgeon-General of the Marine Hospital Service. Those who have escaped from shipwreck and are wet, hungry, and cold are provided with dry clothing, warmed, fed, lodged, and cared for until they are able to leave.

RESTORING THE APPARENTLY DROWNED TO LIFE.

The method adopted for restoring the apparently drowned is formulated into rules which each member of the crew commits to memory. In drill he is required to repeat these and afterwards illustrate them by manipulations upon one of his comrades. The medicine chest is also opened, and he is examined as to the use of its contents.

The dry clothing is taken from the supply constantly kept on hand at the different stations by the Women's National Relief Association, an organization established to afford relief to sufferers from disasters of every kind. The libraries at the stations are from the donations of the Seamen's Friend Society and sundry benevolent persons. The food is prepared by the keepers or the station mess, who are reimbursed by the recipients if they have the means, or by the government.

The life-saving service is attached to the treasury department. The sea and lake coasts of the United States have an extent of more than ten thousand miles, and are divided into thirteen life-saving districts, each under the immediate supervision of a district superintendent. The chief officer of the service is the general superintendent, who has general charge of it and of all administrative matters connected with it. An inspector from the Revenue Marine Service visits each station monthly during the "active season," which is ten months, from August 1 to June 1, and examines and practices the crews in their duties. On his first visit, after the opening of the stations each year, if any are found not up to the standard, they are promptly dropped from the service. The district superintendents are promoted from the corps of keepers, and must be residents of the respective districts for which they are chosen, and are rigidly examined as to their professional familiarity with the line of coast embraced within the district and the use of life-boats and all other life-saving apparatus.

The keeper of each station has direct control of all its affairs, and as his position is one of the most important of the service, the selection is made with the greatest care.

The indispensable qualifications are that he shall be a man of good character and habits, not less than twenty-one and not over forty-five

A RESCUED SHIPWRECKED CREW.

years of age, with sufficient education to be able to transact the business connected with the station, be able bodied, physically sound, and a master of boatcraft and surfing.

No difficulty is found in filling vacancies that occur among the keepers, as they must be promoted from the ranks of the surfmen, and the merits of all the surfmen, having been ascertained by inspection, drill, and active service, are on record. The keepers are required to reside at their stations all the year round, and are entrusted with the care, custody, and government of the station and property. They are captains of their crews, exercise absolute control in matters of discipline, lead the men, and share their perils on all occasions of

WEEKLY TRANSCRIPT OF JOURNAL.

FORM 1809.

..................................Station.   District No.................................

CONDITION OF THE SURF.			
MIDNIGHT.	SUNRISE.	NOON.	SUNSET.
Smooth......	Smooth......	Smooth......	Smooth......
Light........	Light........	Light........	Light........
Moderate....	Moderate....	Moderate....	Moderate....
Strong	Strong.......	Strong........	Strong.......
Rough.......	Rough..	Rough.......	Rough.......
High	High	High	High ....
Very high...	Very high...	Very high...	Very high...

☞ The keeper will make a cross immediately after the word indicating the condition of the surf at midnight, sunrise, noon, and sunset.

Sunday,..........................., 190

Direction and force of wind, and state of weather at midnight,............ ....

Direction and force of wind, and state of weather at sunrise, ...

Direction and force of wind, and state of weather at noon, ...

Direction and force of wind, and state of weather at sunset,........... ....

ENTER THE READING OF BAROMETER AND THERMOMETER AT MIDNIGHT, SUNRISE, NOON, AND SUNSET.

Barometer — Midnight,   ; Sunrise,   ; Noon,   ; Sunset,
Thermometer — Midnight,   ; Sunrise,   ; Noon,   ; Sunset,

(Fill in, in the blank spaces below, the names of the patrolmen or watch, the names of the patrolmen met, and the name of the station the latter were from.)

PATROL.

, midnight to 4 A. M., met	, from	Station.
, midnight to 4 A. M., met	, ,,	,,
, 4 A. M. to sunrise, met	, ,,	,,
, 4 A. M. to sunrise, met	, ,,	,,
, sunset to 8 P. M., met	, ,,	,,
, sunset to 8 P. M., met	, ,,	,,
, 8 P. M. to midnight, met	, ,,	,,
, 8 P. M. to midnight, met	, ,,	,,

Is the house thoroughly clean ?
Is the house in good repair ?
Is the apparatus in good condition ?
Was any member of the crew (including keeper) absent on liberty, if so, who, and from what hour to what hour ?
Was any one absent on twenty-four hours' leave, if so, who ?
Was any one absent for other cause, if so, who, and why ?
Name of substitute: in place of   , surfman.

(Fill in the number of vessels of each class that have passed the station this day.)

Ships,   barks,   brigs,   schooners,   steamers,   sloops,

GENERAL REMARKS.

(Under this head are to be stated all transactions relating to house or service.)

COPY OF DAILY JOURNAL KEPT BY THE KEEPERS OF THE LIFE-SAVING STATIONS.

rescue, always taking the steering oar when the boats are used, and directing all operations with the other apparatus.

The keeper and six men constitute the regular crew at each of the stations on Cape Cod, except at the Monomoy Station, where the regular crew is seven men. An additional man called "the winter man" is added to all stations on December 1 of each year, so that during the most rigorous part of the season one man, at least, may be left ashore to assist in launching and beaching of the surf-boat, and to have charge of the station and perform the extra work that winter weather necessitates.

The life-saving crews are selected from able-bodied and experienced surfmen after the rigid examination required by the department.

SURFMAN GAGE, ORLEANS STATION,
Dressed for cold night, with time clock, beach lantern, and coston signal.

The surfmen, in addition to being obliged to pass a rigid physical examination before they can enter the service, must also pass a similar examination yearly before the opening of the active season. No matter how long they may have been in the service, the hardships they have suffered, the perils they have faced, or the great deeds of heroism they have performed, if they are found not to be physically sound they are dropped from the service, ruined in health, without the slightest compensation for the years of faithful service.

The profession of a surfman is entirely different from that of a sailor, being only acquired by coast fishermen and wreckers after years of experience in passing in and out through the surf. The method of selecting the life-saving crews has resulted in securing the most skilful and fearless surfmen, whose gallant deeds of heroism have made them famous throughout the land. Upon original entry into the service a surfman must be a citizen of the United States, not over forty-five years of age.

He is examined as to his expertness in the management of boats and the use of other life-saving apparatus, and matters of that character. He signs articles by which he agrees to reside at the station continuously during the active season, to perform such duties as may be required of him by the regulations and by his superior officers, and also to hold himself in readiness for service during the inactive season if called upon. For this he receives sixty-five dollars per month. For each occasion he is called upon, during the two months' inactive season, he receives three dollars.

The district superintendents, inspectors, keepers, and crews, the law says, are to be selected "solely with reference to their fitness and without reference to their political or party affiliations."

STRANDED CLOSE TO SHORE.

Every time a wreck occurs the keepers are required to make out and forward to the department a wreck report, containing answers to a great number of pertinent questions.

If a life is lost the law requires that a thorough investigation be instituted with a view of ascertaining the circumstances, and whether the fatality was due to any neglect or misconduct on the part of the service. Any misconduct or incompetency at other times is likewise subject to rigid investigation. The results of the investigations into the circumstances of loss of life are fully set out in the annual reports of the service, which the general superintendent is required to make.

Life savers, disabled in the line of duty, are retained upon the pay-rolls during the continuance of their disability, not to exceed one year, though in certain cases the period may be extended upon recommendation for a greater period, but not more than two years. In case of their death from service or from disease contracted in the line of duty, their widows and children under sixteen years of age are entitled to be paid during a period of two years the same amount that the husband or father would have received.

In addition to saving the lives of the imperiled, an important part of the duty of the life savers is that of saving property. The amount of property saved annually by these guardians of the coast largely exceeds the cost of maintenance of the service. The keepers are authorized and required by law to take charge of and protect all such

LIFE SAVERS FLOATING A SCHOONER.

property until claimed by those legally entitled to receive it, or until otherwise directed by the department as to its disposition. The keepers have the powers of the inspectors of customs and faithfully guard the interests of the government in all dutiable wrecked property.

Doubtless the United States Life-Saving Service system appears to be an expensive and elaborate one, but it must be remembered that, putting aside entirely the consideration of the value of human life, which is beyond computation, it saves many times its cost in property alone, and that it fulfils the functions usually allotted to several different agencies. It rescues the shipwrecked by both the principal methods which humane ingenuity has devised for that purpose, and which, in some countries, are practiced separately by two distinct organizations; it furnishes them the subsequent succor which elsewhere would be afforded by shipwrecked mariners' societies; it guards the lives of persons in peril or of drowning by falling into the water from piers and wharves in the harbors of populous cities, an office usually performed by humane societies; it nightly patrols the dangerous coast for the early discovery of wrecks and the hastening of relief, thus increasing the chances of rescue, and shortening by hours intense physical suffering and the terrible agony of suspense; it places over peculiarly dangerous points upon the rivers and lakes a sentry prepared to send instant relief to those who

THETA, STRANDED IN A BAD PLACE.

incautiously or recklessly incur the hazard of capsizing in boats; it conducts to places of safety those imperiled in their homes by the torrents of flood, and conveys food to those imprisoned in their homes by inundation and threatened by famine; it annually saves, unaided, hundreds of stranded vessels, with their cargoes, from total or partial destruction, and assists in saving scores of others; it protects wrecked property after landing from the ravage of the elements and the rapine of plunderers; it extricates vessels unwarily caught in perilous positions; it averts numerous disasters by its flashing signals of warning to vessels standing in danger; it assists the custom service in collecting the revenues of the government; it pickets the coast with a guard, which prevents smuggling, and, in time of war, surprise by hostile forces, which makes the service unlike all other organizations established for similar purposes.

The distinction of having founded and created the United States Life-Saving Service having been the subject of much discussion in recent years, General Superintendent Kimball, in his report to the Secretary of the Treasury as to the claims of W. A. Newell, as the originator of the system of the Life-Saving Service of the United States, in conclusion states as follows: —

"The fact is, the credit of originating and developing the United States Life-Saving Service cannot truthfully be awarded to any single individual.

"In Congress and out of Congress many men have contributed, some

BEACH COMBERS WAITING TO STRIP THE WRECKED VESSEL.

in a great and some in a less degree to the success of its fortunes. To even write down the names of the legislators in both houses of Congress, who have been its advocates and champions, and to refer ever so briefly to their valuable assistance, would occupy much space and require considerable research, but there occurred to me at once as conspicuous among the host of its promoters, Senators Hannibal H. Hamlin, O. D. Conger, W. E. Kenna, W. J. Sewell, and William P. Frye, and Representatives S. S. Cox, Charles B. Roberts, John Lynch, James W. Cobert, and Jesse J. Yeates. Presidents of the United States and various Secretaries of the Treasury have promoted its welfare. Many officers of the life-saving service also, as well as officers detailed to it from the Revenue Cutter Service, have, from time to time, suggested and assisted to carry into effect important improvements.

"The life-saving service was not designed and laid out at one stroke, in a single comprehensive plan, as an architect designs a building, or a military genius, perhaps, devised a scheme of army organization, but its system and development have been accomplished step by step, day teaching unto day the necessity and wisdom of each successive measure of progress."

CAPT. BENJAMIN C. SPARROW.

Capt. Benjamin C. Sparrow, superintendent of the second life-saving district, was born in Orleans, Oct. 9, 1839. He is a lineal descendant of Richard Sparrow, who came over in the ship *Ann*, landing at Plymouth. When a boy he always accompanied his father, a well-known life saver and wrecker, to the shipwrecks that occurred along the coast, and at an early age became familiar with the scenes of disaster from which the shores of Cape Cod have become noted.

In those early days, long before the establishment of United States life-saving stations on Cape Cod, volunteer crews responded to the calls for assistance when there was a wreck along the coast. There were others who engaged in the work of saving lives and of wrecking, or assisting distressed vessels, and they were known as "beach combers."

Captain Sparrow was a "beach comber" for many years, and relates thrilling and interesting incidents that occurred during his experience. After finishing his education in the public schools of his native town, he taught in the public schools in the adjoining town of Eastham.

He entered Phillips Academy to prepare himself for the legal profession, and was a student there at the outbreak of the Civil War. The war had hardly begun, however, before he left college, and enlisted in the regular army, in the engineer battalion attached to the headquarters of the Army of the Potomac, serving in this capacity until 1864. During his term of service he endured much hardship, being a prisoner at Belle Isle in the summer of 1862.

At the close of the war he returned to his home in East Orleans, where he has since resided. On Dec. 25, 1866, he married Miss Eunice S. Felton, of Shutesbury, Mass.

He has been connected with the United States Life-Saving Service for thirty years, or since the time of its reorganization, his appointment as district superintendent being a part of the plan adopted by the government to stamp out the evils which existed in the service at the time.

Captain Sparrow in the thirty years in which he has been superintendent of the second district has been actively engaged in the arduous duties of his calling, and to his efforts is due the success in securing the discipline and efficiency in this hazardous service in the district under his charge.

His home is connected by telephone with all the stations along the

CAPT. B. C. SPARROW, DISTRICT SUPERINTENDENT UNITED STATES LIFE-SAVING STATION.

shores of the Cape, and the moment a wreck is reported to him he is away to the scene.

Ofttimes he has been obliged to travel many miles on foot in the teeth of a raging gale and driving storm to reach the scene of a disaster, yet he has attended nearly every wreck that has taken place along the shores of Cape Cod during the past thirty years.

The veteran captain has often shared the hardships and braved the perils with the life savers in their work along the beaches, and the

The Life Savers of Cape Cod.

hardships of thirty years have left their deep imprint upon him. The night that the schooner *Calvin B. Orcutt* was wrecked on Chatham bars, Captain Sparrow suffered such hardship going to the scene that his eyesight has since been seriously impaired.

The life-saving department recognized Captain Sparrow's ability from the first by appointing him on the board of experts to examine new appliances and methods proposed for use by the department.

This position he has filled with great credit to himself and to the betterment of the department to the present.

Captain Sparrow has always taken an active interest in the affairs of

A DERELICT CAST ASHORE.

his town, and his fellow-citizens have honored him from time to time with public offices within their gift. To the life savers of Cape Cod Captain Sparrow has ever been a staunch friend.

HIGHLAND STATION.

This station derives its name from the Highlands of Cape Cod which are in the immediate vicinity, and is one of the original nine stations built on Cape Cod in 1872. It is seven-eighths of a mile west of Cape Cod Highland Light, and about one and one-half miles from the North Truro village.

Its approximate position as obtained from the latest coast survey charts is latitude north 42° 02′ 55″, longitude west 70° 04′ 20″. Shoals run parallel with the shores at this station, and many appalling disasters have occurred there since the station has been established. The surfmen exchange checks with the surfmen from the High Head Station on the west patrol, which is about one and three-quarter miles, and with the surfmen from the Pamet River Station on the east patrol, which is about two and one-half miles. On the east patrol the surfmen are unable at times to follow the beach, the tides forcing them to grope their way along the tops of the cliffs, which, in many places, rise one hundred feet above the level of the sea. So steep are the cliffs at points along the east patrol, that the surfmen have ropes extending from the top to the bottom by which they are able to reach the top when driven from the beach by the tides. In attempting to climb one of these steep cliffs on a stormy night a few years ago, Henry Baldwin,

HIGHLAND STATION.

a substitute at this station, had the bank break under him, and falling to the beach below, a distance of nearly fifty feet, fractured his hip and received multiple injuries. When the unfortunate surfman did not return to the station at the appointed time, a surfman was sent out to search for him. No trace of him could be found, however, and at four o'clock in the morning Captain Worthen called all hands, and after a search of a few hours, the injured surfman was found on the beach attempting to crawl to the station. This shows one of the perils which confront the surfmen attached to this station. John Francis, a surfman, who, after eighteen years of service at this station, was forced to resign from it on account of injury to his eyesight, had a narrow escape from death while a member of this station crew. Francis was attempting to make his way along the beach to a point where he could climb to the top of the cliffs. The sea was running high, and the great undertow catching Francis, threw him down and carried him far out from the shore. He struggled desperately, and by the merest chance succeeded in making his way out of the surf, when thrown upon the shore by a mountainous wave. He was more dead than alive when he reached the station. Surfman William Paine, of this station, had a fearful experience during a blinding snowstorm. Paine got lost, his eyes becoming frostbitten so that he could not open them. He walked about all night in a little

NEAR THE HIGHLAND STATION.

grove of pine woods to keep from freezing, and was found the following day by his comrades.

There are three surf-boats at this station, two for active service, one for drilling the crew, two beach carts with full sets of apparatus, and a life-car. One of the surf-boats and a beach cart are kept in a house near the shore. "Nellie," a horse owned by Captain Worthen, is employed at the station during the winter months. Cats and dogs are the pets of the surfmen, a number of them living about the station.

Captain Worthen has been keeper of this station since it was placed in commission, a period of over thirty years. During that time there is a record of twenty-seven wrecks within the province of the station. The records as to the number of persons taken ashore is not plain, although it is certain that one hundred and fifty have been rescued by Captain Worthen and his crew.

Only one crew in the whole history of the station has been rescued by means of the breeches-buoy, the crew, ten in number, of the British bark *Kate Harding*, from Barbadoes, which stranded during a fierce gale and dangerous sea, were thus safely taken ashore. The bark became a total wreck.

CAPT. EDWIN P. WORTHEN.

Capt. Edwin P. Worthen, keeper of the Highland Life-Saving Station, has the distinction of being the oldest keeper in point of years of service, not only on Cape Cod, but in the United States. He has been

ALONG THE SHORE AT HIGHLAND LIGHT.
Showing steps which life savers climb when driven to the top of the cliffs by the seas.

in the life-saving service for more than thirty years, and has been the keeper of the Highland Station since the station's establishment. He is a native of Charlestown, Mass., having been born in that city sixty-five years ago, or July 27, 1837, to be exact.

Captain Worthen is indeed a warrior of the sea, a triumphant fighter of the storms that sweep the coasts of Cape Cod, a life saver who has witnessed some of the most awful scenes of terror at time of shipwreck, and heroically rescued seafarers from the very jaws of death.

When but eight years of age, Captain Worthen went to sea as cook on a fishing and coasting vessel, continuing to follow the sea in one capacity or another until he was thirty-five years of age, when he was appointed keeper of the Highland Station.

Not one of the original crew of the Highland Station is in the service at present, save the veteran keeper Captain Worthen. For thirty years he has made the station which he helped to build his home, and has been a faithful and vigilant guardian of the coast. Skilled in the art of handling boats through the surf, absolutely fearless when duty calls, he has an enviable record as a life saver. Under his watch-

CAPT. EDWIN P. WORTHEN, KEEPER OF HIGHLAND STATION.

ful eye, careful guidance, and discipline, the members of his crew have been trained to perfection in the art and science of managing boats in the most riotous waters, and are ever ready to follow their keeper.

In his thirty years of service as keeper on the dangerous coast of Cape Cod, he has assisted at nearly all the wrecks that have occurred in the region of the " Highlands," yet he never received an injury of any kind in that whole time. Captain Worthen has always taken a deep interest in the welfare of the life savers, and his associates of the Surfman's Mutual Benefit Association of the United States have honored him with the office of chairman of the District Committee.

While Captain Worthen has witnessed many changes in the service along the shores of Cape Cod, the shifting treacherous sand bars near his station, however, still remain as a menace to the mariner, and continue to levy a fearful tribute on the shipping around Cape Cod. The sands along the coast there are literally strewn with half-buried skeletons of wrecked vessels, while unmarked mounds in the little village graveyards near by, tell a sorrowful tale of the fearful sacrifice of human life. The first wreck which Captain Worthen went to after his appointment as keeper was on Dec. 25, 1872, before the station was built. With volunteers he rescued fourteen men, the whole crew of the German bark *Francis*, which became a total loss. The same night another vessel, the *Peruvian*, was lost on the coast, and her crew of twenty-eight perished. The captain of the *Francis* died two days later, and was buried near the Highland Station, Captain Worthen caring for his grave ever since.

Captain Worthen enjoys good health, despite his age and the great number of years he has served as a life saver, and seems destined to enjoy a long life. He married Julia E. Francis.

HIGHLAND CREW.

The No. 1 surfman is William P. Paine. He was born in North Truro in 1866, and has been in the life-saving service for twelve years, all of which have been spent at this station. From his boyhood days Surfman Paine was a boatman and fisherman along the shores of Cape Cod, and was well accustomed to braving the hardships and facing the perils that fall to the lot of a life saver. He married Edith L. Hopkins.

The No. 2 surfman is Hiram R. Hatch. He was born in Truro, is forty-four years of age, and has been in the life-saving service for twenty-one years. Surfman Hatch went to sea when a boy, shipping before the mast on a coasting vessel. He followed the sea until he was twenty-three years of age, and was a skilled boatman when he joined the service. In his long years of experience as a surfman he has had many thrilling escapes, and has proved a faithful and able life saver. He married Sarah W. Small, and is the father of a daughter.

The No. 3 surfman is William McFadden. He was born in Provincetown in 1872, and has been a member of this station crew for eight years. He had a wide and varied experience on the water

The Life Savers of Cape Cod.   65

before entering the service, and has made an able and skilled life saver. He married Sarah R. Knowles.

The No. 4 surfman is Manuel F. Oliver. He was born in Provincetown, is twenty-eight years of age, and the youngest member of this station crew. Surfman Oliver has been in the life-saving service two years. He spent one year at the Gay Head Station on Martha's Vineyard. He was a sailor, boatman, and fisherman before entering the service and has made a valued member of Captain Worthen's crew. He married Maggie Morris, and is the father of two children, a daughter and son.

The No. 5 surfman is Antone T. Lucas. He was born in Fayal,

A. T. LUCAS.   M. F. OLIVER.   W. P. PAINE.   H. R. HATCH.
JOHN MARSHALL.   CAPTAIN WORTHEN.   M. FRANCIS.   WM. M. MCFADDEN.
HIGHLAND CREW.

Azore Islands, and is forty-eight years of age. Surfman Lucas has been in the life-saving service for twenty-five years, all of which have been spent at this station. Prior to his entering the service he went to sea on coasting vessels and merchant ships, and for several years he was a whaleman. In his twenty-five years of service as a life saver he has endured much hardship, has faced the greatest peril in the performance of his duty, and is a faithful and fearless warrior of the sea.

The No. 6 surfman is Manuel Frances. He was born in Provincetown, and is thirty-two years of age. Surfman Frances has been in the life-saving service for two years. He was a boatman and fisherman off the shores of Cape Cod for a number of years, and well prepared for the work he is called upon to perform as a life saver. He married Carrie Silva, and is the father of two daughters and one son.

The No. 7 surfman is John Marshall. He was born in St. Georges Fayal, Azore Islands, in 1853. Surfman Marshall has been in the life-saving service for twenty-two years, all of which have been spent at this station. Before he entered the service he spent a number of years on the water as a sailor, boatman, and fisherman. During his long term of service he has had several narrow escapes from death in the performance of duty. Owing to an injury which he received while at work assisting at a wreck, he was incapacitated for duty for a period of six months. Surfman Marshall is an able boatman and a brave and hardy life saver.

CAHOON'S HOLLOW STATION.

The Cahoon's Hollow Station is located on the "back side" of Cape Cod, two and one-half miles east of Wellfleet. The present station replaced the one which was destroyed by fire in February, 1893. The original station was one of the nine that were built on the shores of Cape Cod in 1872. The station's approximate position as obtained from the latest coast survey charts is latitude north 41° 56′ 40″, and its longitude west 69° 55′ 05″.

The surfmen from this station on the north patrol cover a distance of about two and one-half miles, meeting and exchanging checks with

CAHOON'S HOLLOW STATION.

the surfmen from the Pamet River Station. On the south patrol the surfmen have a walk of about four miles, meeting and exchanging checks with the surfmen from the Nauset Station.

The coast at this station is exceedingly dangerous; sunken rips stretch out under the sea and extend along the shore for miles. Owing to the great sand dunes which have been built by the winds, the surfmen are unable to obtain a good observation seaward from the lookout on the station, and the day watches are stationed in a small house on the bluff overlooking the sea.

There are three surf-boats, one dory, two beach carts, breeches-buoys, etc., and one life-car at this station. Two surf-boats and the dory are used for the work of rescue and one for practice. The life-car has never been used save for practice.

At the Cahoon's Hollow Station since Captain Cole has been keeper, sixteen vessels of different types have become stranded on the beach there. On these vessels there was a total of one hundred and twenty-four persons, and of this number but one person was lost. Those saved by Captain Cole and his crew were taken ashore in all kinds of ways, some by the surf-boat, others by the breeches-buoy, and many were dragged through the surf with lines. Charles H. Ashley, of Haverhill, was the only person lost within the patrol of the Cahoon's Hollow Station. He was a member of the crew of the barge *Blackbird*, and was drowned attempting to reach the shore in a small boat. Of the sixteen vessels that were cast ashore on the beach ten were a total loss.

CAPT. DANIEL COLE.

Capt. Daniel Cole, keeper of the Cahoon's Hollow Life-Saving Station, was born in Wellfleet in 1844, and has been in the life-saving service ever since it was established on Cape Cod, with the exception of one year. He entered the service when the Cahoon's Hollow Station was manned, and after serving as a surfman for a number of years was appointed keeper twenty-three years ago.

Captain Cole, in addition to being a veteran life saver, is also a veteran of the Civil War. When a boy hardly nine years of age he went to sea, his first trip being to the Grand Banks on a vessel that sailed from Cape Cod. He continued to go to the Grand Banks year after year until he went to the West, and engaged in trading on the Great Lakes. He was a trader on the lakes when the war broke out. He was but nineteen years of age, but of fine physique, strong, healthy, appeared much older, and was readily accepted in the 12th Illinois Regiment, Company K, Second Brigade, 15th Army Corps, and was soon on his way to the front. He participated in numerous engagements, and was with Sherman on his "march to the sea."

When his term of enlistment expired he was discharged, at Louisville, Ky., and at once returned to his home on Cape Cod. He again went fishing to the Banks, continuing until the life-saving service was extended to Cape Cod, when he was prevailed upon to join the new crew at Cahoon's Hollow. He continued to serve as a surfman for a number of years, joining the station crew at the close of each fishing season. One year, while he was master of a fishing vessel, he remained

CAPT. DANIEL COLE, CAHOON'S HOLLOW STATION.

out of the service. The following season he joined the station when the crew went on duty, and has been at the station continuously since that time. William Newcombe, who was placed in charge of the station when it was manned, resigned after a few years, and Captain Cole was placed in command. As a surfman, Captain Cole had shown rare judgment and exceptional skill in the work of saving life and property, and his promotion to keeper of such an important station was a merited reward. He has made an enviable record as a life saver since keeper, but one life having been lost within the patrol of his station since he took charge. Disasters are frequent along the shore near his station, and the crew have made many heroic rescues, and had numerous thrilling escapes in devotion to their duty. One of the worst wrecks that have occurred within the province of the station happened on Dec. 31, 1890, when the schooner *Smuggler* became a total loss. The vessel struck during a furious gale, and was discovered by one of the surfmen about four o'clock in the morning. Running to the station, a distance of about two miles, the surfman aroused the keeper and crew, and all hands started for the wreck in the teeth of the gale, with the beach apparatus

PANCHITA, DRIVEN ASHORE AT PROVINCETOWN.

in a wagon drawn by the station horse. The whirlwinds of sand sweeping along the shore blinded the men, and the horse at times refused to go. After much hardship, but with little delay, Captain Cole and his crew reached the scene. The fifteen men, the crew of the vessel, had been driven into the rigging, and the craft was fast breaking up and moving along the shore. With great despatch a shot was fired over the vessel, the breeches-buoy was put in working order, and the men pulled through the surf from the stranded vessel to the shore. The life savers suffered terribly from the cold, and the rescued crew were nearly dead when they reached the shore. As the last man was pulled out of the surf, the vessel went to pieces, not a vestige being left to mark the spot where the disaster took place.

Captain Cole maintains a high standard of efficiency and discipline at his station, and has a crew of fearless and skilled life savers. Captain Cole married Harriet Blodget, and is the father of two sons. He is a member of the J. C. Freeman Post, G. A. R., No. 55, of Provincetown, the Surfmen's Mutual Benefit Association, the Royal Arcanum, and the Adams Lodge, F. A. M.

CAHOON'S HOLLOW STATION CREW.

The No. 1 surfman is Freeman W. Atwood. He was born in Wellfleet in 1846, and has been in the life-saving service for twenty-five years, all of which have been at this station. Before entering the service Surfman Atwood was a fisherman and coastwise sailor. He went to sea when a boy, and from his long experience as a fisherman and sailor along the shores of the Cape was well prepared for the work of a life saver. In all his years of experience he has never met with serious mishap. He has seen much hardship as a member of this crew and can be relied upon to unflinchingly face the greatest perils in the performance of his duty. He married Lucy N. Rich, and is the father of three boys.

The No. 2 surfman is Eugene O. Young. He was born in Yarmouth Port and is forty-nine years of age. Surfman Young has been a life saver for nineteen years, joining this station when he entered the service. He was a boatman, fisherman, and coastwise sailor before entering the service, and has made a valued member of the station crew, as he is a tried and true life saver. Surfman Young has assisted at all the wrecks that have taken place at the station during his term of service, and has suffered much hardship and had many perilous adventures within that period. He married Susan A. Rich, and has a family of two girls and one boy.

The No. 3 surfman is Edward Lombard. He was born in Truro in 1865, and has been in the life-saving service for twelve years, three at the Pamet River Station, the remaining nine at this station. Surfman Lombard was a fisherman and boatman before he entered the service. He saw much active service while a member of the Pamet River Station, and has always proven himself a brave and skilled life saver. He married Nellie Howes, and has a family of four boys.

The No. 4 surfman is Stanley M. Fisher. He was born in Nantucket in 1877, and is serving his first year as a life saver. Surfman Fisher, after spending a few years as a boatman and fisherman along the shores of Nantucket, went to Texas, where he worked on a stock ranch. Tiring of this kind of a life, he enlisted in the regular army, Company K, Sixth Regiment, and went with his regiment to the Philippine Islands, remaining there until the expiration of his term of service. Fisher, with his regiment, was stationed on Negroes Island for one year, and also at Panay for a year. He took part in six hot battles and several minor engagements with the Philippines, but escaped without the slightest injury. He was a member of a volunteer crew which rescued a crew from a sunken vessel in Vineyard Haven Harbor during the gale of November, 1898, receiving gold and silver medals as a recognition of his bravery.

Fisher is an expert boatman, and under the guidance of Captain Cole he cannot fail to become an able and skilful life saver.

CAPTAIN COLE.   EUGENE O. YOUNG.   STANLEY M. FISHER.
FREEMAN W. ATWOOD.   EDWARD LOMBARD.   JAMES LOPES.
CAHOON'S HOLLOW CREW.

The No. 5 surfman is James Lopes. He was born in Provincetown in 1866, and is serving his first year as a life saver, having joined the crew at this station in August, 1902. Prior to his joining the service he was a boat fisherman along the shores of the Cape. He was a member of a volunteer crew which rescued a crew from a vessel wrecked in Provincetown Harbor during the November gale of 1898, and received a medal in recognition of his bravery. He had a wide experience in boating and is possessed of the qualities necessary to make an able life saver. He married Minnie Rogers, and is the father of one child, a daughter.

The No. 6 surfman is Clarence L. Burch. He was born in Provincetown in 1875. Surfman Burch is a new man in the service, having joined in the service in December, 1902. He had been a boatman and fisherman along the shores of the Cape for a number of years, and also a coastwise sailor. He went with a party of prospectors to the Klondike gold region, but remained there a short time, returning to Cape Cod to engage in fishing. He is skilled in the art of managing boats in all kinds of weather, and well qualified for the work of a life saver. He married Dorothy McKenzie, and is the father of two girls.

The No. 7 surfman is Charles H. Jennings. He was born in Provincetown in 1878, and is serving his first year as a regular surfman. Surfman Jennings was a fisherman and boatman before he entered the service, and had also substituted as a surfman at the

ICEBERGS ALONG THE SHORE AT PEAKED HILL.

High Head Station, under Captain Kelley. He will receive careful training under Captain Cole, and will, no doubt, make a skilled and fearless life saver. He married Edith J. Rogers.

PEAKED HILL BARS STATION.

The Peaked Hill Bars Station is another of the original nine stations which were erected on Cape Cod in 1872. A more bleak or dangerous stretch of coast can hardly be found in the United States than at this station. The coast near the station rightly bears the name "Ocean Graveyard." Sunken rips stretch far out under the sea at this place, ever ready to grasp the keels of the ships that sail down upon them, and many appalling disasters have taken place there. There are two lines of bars that lie submerged off the shore at Peaked Hill Bars Station, the outer and inner bars they are called. They run parallel with the coast line for a distance of about six miles. The outer bars lie about fourteen hundred yards offshore, the inner bars about six hundred. These bars are ever shifting, and the depth of water on them varies in accordance. It is not often that vessels are wrecked on the outer bars, although they often strike there and are driven over them only to meet with destruction on the inner bars. The surfmen of this station have a patrol of about two miles east and west, meeting and exchanging checks on the westward patrol with the surfmen from Race Point Station on the eastward with the surfmen of the High Head Station.

When the station was erected there was a long stretch of low beach

PEAKED HILL BARS STATION.

between it and the shore, but now sand dunes made by the action of the wind shut off all view of the ocean except from the lookout tower on the station. It is at this station that the effect of the flying sand upon the glass in the windows is plainly seen, the whirlwinds of sand having made them as rough as if they had been dipped in acid, and almost shutting out the light of day. This effect of the sand in destroying the transparency of the window-panes is an object of curiosity and never-failing wonder to visitors. On the bluff overlooking the ocean the crew have erected a small building, where the day watches keep a lookout and members of the crew spend some of their leisure moments.

The station is located two and one-half miles east of Provincetown village, and its approximate position as obtained from the latest coast survey charts is latitude north 42° 04′ 40″, longitude 70° 09′ 50″. From Provincetown the road to the station crosses the great sand deserts for which that region is noted.

This station is supplied with two surf-boats, one four oared, the other five, two sets of beach apparatus, breeches-buoys, guns, etc., and a practice boat.

Captain Cook and his crew of the Peaked Hill Bars Station have taken twenty-five persons ashore in their surf-boat, and one in the breeches-buoy since Captain Cook assumed charge of the station.

THE SAND DUNES ON THE WAY TO PEAKED HILL BARS STATION.

The following vessels, which struck on the Peaked Hill Bars, became a total loss: *Willie H. Higgins*, *Albert L. Butler*, *Cathie C. Berry*, *Kate L. Robinson*, and *Jennie C. May*.

Seven men and one woman were taken ashore from the *Higgins*. The captain and one sailor were washed ashore from the schooner *Albert L. Butler*, which was wrecked during the memorable November gale of '98, and one man was taken off by the breeches-buoy, while two others were taken ashore after the tide went down.

The schooner *Cathie Berry* stranded during a terrific gale. The life savers launched their boat and went to her only to find her abandoned. The schooner *Helen* came ashore during a bad time; the life savers went to her in their boat, but none of the crew came ashore.

The schooner *Kate L. Robinson* carried a crew of seven men, and all were rescued by Captain Cook and his crew in their surf-boat. The crew of the *Theta*, seven in number, together with a woman passenger, were also taken ashore in the surf-boat, as were two members of the crew of the *Jennie C. May*.

CAPTAIN COOK. PEAKED HILL BARS.

Capt. William W. Cook, keeper of the Peaked Hill Bars Station, one of the most dangerous of all, was born in Provincetown, within sight

CAPT. WILLIAM W. COOK, KEEPER OF PEAKED HILL BARS STATION.

of his station, Nov. 3, 1852. He has been in the life-saving service for twenty years, fourteen years as a surfman and six as keeper at this station. When a boy he evidenced great love for boats, and after leaving school, until he entered the life-saving service, he spent nearly all his time at sea. He was first in the merchant service, but later joined the fleet of whaling vessels that cruised on the north and south Atlantic grounds, gaining a wide experience as a whaleman, and becoming thoroughly familiar with the handling of boats under the most trying conditions and roughest weather. When he decided to enter the life-saving service the department was glad to secure him, and as an evidence of their faith in his ability, they assigned him to the dangerous Peaked Hill Bars Station, under the late Capt. Isaac G. Fisher.

For fourteen years Captain Cook patrolled the beaches and faithfully performed the duties of a surfman, and then succeeded Captain Fisher as keeper, when the latter was transferred to the Wood End Station. In all his years of experience, both as a surfman and keeper of this station, Captain Cook has never had his boat capsized, has never been overboard from his boat, and has never lost or had a member of his crew seriously injured in the performance of duty.

Of all the wrecks which Captain Cook and his crew have gone to, one of the most hazardous undertakings was at the wreck of the three-masted schooner *Willie H. Higgins*, in March, 1898, from which they rescued seven men and one woman in the surf-boat. At the wreck of the schooner *Theta*, Captain Cook and his crew made a most daring rescue of her crew of seven, and the captain's wife. The rescue was made in the surf-boat in a riotous sea that threatened to engulf the boat and drown both rescued and rescuers. The thrilling rescue was witnessed by a vast multitude that had assembled on the beach, and a mighty cheer was sent up as willing hands pulled the surf-boat out of the maddened waters onto the beach.

Captain Cook uses a twenty-one foot steering oar when going to a wreck in the surf-boat, and to this he attributes his great success in handling the craft under the worst conditions of wind or wave. The steering oar is the same kind as he used when a whaleman. That he is skilled in the use of it is evidenced by the enviable record he has made since he has been keeper of the station. He is a warrior of the sea who knows no fear when duty calls, and who is ever ready to put off from the beach to aid distressed seafarers, when it is possible for a boat to live. He married Annie Young Snow, and is the father of a daughter.

PEAKED HILL BARS STATION CREW.

The No. 1 surfman is Levi A. Kelley. He was born in Provincetown, and is forty years of age. Surfman Kelley entered the service in 1884, and was assigned to this station. He is an expert boatman, and the life of a life saver has not the least terror for him. He followed the sea for a number of years as a fisherman and sailor, and became well accustomed to the hardships similar to those of a surfman before he joined the service. He married Nona B. Lewis, and is the father of a boy.

The Life Savers of Cape Cod.

The No. 2 surfman is Benjamin S. Henderson. He was born in Wellfleet in 1855, and has been a member of this station crew for seventeen years, or since he entered the service. Surfman Henderson came from a sea-going family, and took naturally to the hard and perilous work that life savers are called upon to perform. He followed the sea for a number of years before entering the service. He married Mary Dears, and is the father of two girls and two boys.

The No. 3 surfman is James F. Fish. Surfman Fish was born in East Boston in 1853. When a young man he went to sea, making a number of trips on fishing vessels, and later entering the merchant

LEVY KELLEY.   WM. D. CARLOS.   CHAS. HIGGINS.   BENJ. R. KELLEY.
JAS. F. FISH.   CAPT. W. W. COOK.   WM. E. SILVEY.
PEAKED HILL BARS CREW.

service. He entered the life-saving service in 1881, being assigned to this station, and has served faithfully in the capacity of a surfman for nearly twenty-two years. Surfman Fish served his apprenticeship as a life saver under the late Capt. Isaac G. Fisher. He has had many thrilling adventures and narrow escapes from death in the service. He is an expert boatman and as fearless a surfman as patrols the shores of Cape Cod. He married Mary L. Enos.

The No. 4 surfman is William D. Carlos. He was born in Provincetown in 1870, and has been in the life-saving service for five years. Surfman Carlos went to sea when he was seventeen years of age, engaging in boating and fishing from that time until he entered the service. He was first assigned to the Chatham Station, where he remained for one year, being transferred to this station in 1898. He gained a thorough knowledge of handling boats in the roughest water while a fisherman, and was well fitted for the work of a surfman along the dangerous coast of Cape Cod. He married Matilda B. Travis, and is the father of a boy.

The No. 5 surfman is Charles A. Higgins. He was born in Provincetown in 1862, and has been in the life-saving service for seven years. Surfman Higgins followed the vocation of a boat fisherman from the time he was a young man until he joined the crew at Peaked Hill Bars. He is an expert boatman and a brave and faithful surfman. He married Bessie L. Bangs.

The No. 6 surfman is William E. Sylvia. He was born in Provincetown, and is thirty-two years of age. Surfman Sylvia is a new man, but has had a wide experience as a sailor and fisherman, and possesses the other qualities that go to make a successful surfman. He married Louise Smith.

The No. 7 surfman is Benjamin R. Kelley. He was born in Truro, and is fifty-seven years of age, the oldest surfman, in point of years, at this station. Surfman Kelley was assigned to this station when he entered the service eighteen years ago, and has remained a member of the crew ever since. He followed the sea for a number of years before entering the service, and is an old and tried surfman.

ALONG THE SHORE AT PEAKED HILL BARS.

RACE POINT STATION.

This station is one of the original nine stations erected on Cape Cod in 1872, and was manned in the winter of 1873. The station is one and five-eighths miles east of Race Point, from which it derives its name. Its approximate position as obtained from the latest coast survey charts is latitude north 42° 04' 45", longitude west 70° 13' 15". From Provincetown the station is about four miles distant, and easy of access over a highway across the sand dunes. The coast at Race Point is very treacherous, and has been the scene of many wrecks. The tides run past the point with great velocity, and vessels are fre-

RACE POINT STATION.

quently swept to destruction on the sunken rips which lie along the coast there.

The surfmen of this station go over a patrol westward of two and one-half miles, and eastward about one and three-quarters miles. On the eastward patrol the surfmen meet and exchange checks with the surfmen from Peaked Hill Bars Station; on the westward patrol the surfmen use a time clock, as "Race Run" so called, an inlet through the beach, prevents them from meeting the surfmen from Wood End Station. The station is supplied with three surf-boats of the Race Point model, two beach carts, with guns, breeches-buoys, etc., and a life-car

Ninety-two vessels, of all descriptions, have met with disaster near this station since Capt. "Sam" Fisher has been keeper. On these vessels there were over six hundred seafarers, including two women. Of this number of persons taken ashore, thirty-seven were landed by the breeches-buoy, the surf-boat being employed to bring the others that were saved to the shore.

"Nigger," the horse which is on duty at the Race Point Station, is a noble and intelligent animal. When storms are sweeping the coast, "Nigger" shows a restlessness that is not dispelled until fair weather again prevails. As the surfmen return from their patrol at night, "Nigger" always gives evidence in some way or another that he is awake and ready for duty. "Nigger" takes kindly to the work of dragging the heavy beach apparatus and surf-boat through the sands,

NIGGER, THE HORSE KEPT AT RACE POINT STATION.

and responds to the call "ship ashore" as lively as the surfmen. "Nigger" is the pet of all the surfmen, and seems to enjoy having visitors call to see him.

CAPT. SAMUEL O. FISHER.

Capt. Samuel O. Fisher, keeper of the Race Point Life-Saving Station, was born in Provincetown in 1861, and has been in the life-saving service twenty-three years, eight of which he spent as surfman at Peaked Hill Bars Station and fifteen as keeper of this station. "Sam" Fisher came from a seafaring family and is a near relative of the late Isaac G. Fisher, a noted life saver. He went to sea as a sailor on a coasting vessel when a young man. He left the coastwise trade to go tow boating, which he followed for a short time, when he again entered the coastwise trade. He was also a fisherman and boatman off the shores of Cape Cod. He entered the life-saving service when nineteen years of age, being assigned to the Peaked Hill Bars Station under the late Captain Atkins. He was then an experienced boatman, strong and robust. He had been a member of the station crew but a short time when he came near losing his life in a terrible tragedy that took place on the bars near the station.

It was at the time the sloop *C. M. Trumbull* stranded on Peaked Hill Bars. Captain Atkins and his brave crew had pulled out to the

CAPT. "SAM" O. FISHER, KEEPER OF RACE POINT STATION.

stranded sloop and was about to effect the rescue of the imperiled crew when the surf-boat was capsized, throwing all hands into the raging sea. Captain Atkins and two members of the crew perished, Fisher and two others managing to reach the shore after a desperate struggle. After the death of Captain Atkins, the late Capt. Isaac G. Fisher was prevailed upon to take charge of the station. Capt. "Sam" Fisher remained as surfman under Capt. Isaac Fisher until he was appointed keeper of the Race Point Station, succeeding John W. Young.

From his experience at Peaked Hill Bars Station Capt. "Sam" Fisher was well fitted for the arduous duties of keeper of the Race Point Station. During the fifteen years that he has been keeper of the Race Point Station he has led his crew to deeds of great heroism. He has had many narrow escapes from serious injury and death in the performance of his duty, and was once obliged to retire for a period of fifty days on account of injuries received while working on a wrecked schooner. Once he was obliged to swim ashore from an overturned boat, and several times he has narrowly escaped losing his life going

LIFE SAVER STARTING OUT ON THE SUNSET WATCH FROM RACE POINT STATION.

to wrecks. Lawrence Maddocks, a member of the crew who was thrown out of the boat with Captain Fisher at the time of the wreck of the schooner *Julia Bailey*, died shortly after from the effects of exposure.

He married Myra L. Pierce.

RACE POINT STATION CREW.

The No. 1 surfman is Edwin B. Tyler. He was born in Provincetown, is thirty-two years of age, and has been in the United States Life-Saving Service five years. Prior to his joining the service he engaged in boating and fishing. In this way he obtained a thorough knowledge of the coast about the tip end of the Cape, and became skilled in the management of boats in the surf, all of which has been of great value to him since he entered the service. Surfman Tyler, in the few years that he has been in the service, has had his full share of the hardship that is part of the life of a life saver on Cape Cod. He married Pauline Ryder.

The No. 2 surfman is George H. Burch. Surfman Burch was born in Provincetown fifty years ago, and in point of years of service he is the oldest member of the crew of the Race Point Station. He has been a member of the Race Point Station crew for fifteen years, joining the station when he entered the service. Surfman Burch went to sea when a boy, and followed it until he entered the life-saving service.

FRANK BROWN.   EDWIN B. TYLER.   GEO. H. BURCH.
   MARTIN NELSON.   CAPTAIN FISHER.   JOHN B. BANGS.
RACE POINT CREW.

In addition to being a coastwise sailor, he also went in pursuit of the whale. He is an old and tried life saver who knows no fear, and on whom the fifteen years of hardship has left no visible trace. He married Mary Sylva of Provincetown, and is the father of a son.

The No. 3 surfman is Henry I. Collins. He was born in Truro in 1871. Surfman Collins entered the life-saving service three years ago, being assigned to this station. Before entering the service he had followed the sea as a boatman and fisherman from the time he was a small boy. He is an expert boatman, and was not long in the service before he demonstrated his worth as a life saver. He married Nellie Lombard, and is the father of two girls.

The No. 4 surfman is Frank Brown. Surfman Brown was born in Provincetown in 1866. He joined the life-saving service in 1899, being assigned to the Muskeget Station at Nantucket. After serving there for several months he was transferred to this station. Surfman Brown from his long experience as a fisherman and in the coasting trade is an expert boatman, and also possesses all the other qualifications necessary to make a life saver. He married Margaret Sullivan of Provincetown.

The No. 5 man is John B. Bangs. He was born in Provincetown and is twenty-nine years of age. Surfman Bangs has been in the service seven years. He was first assigned to the High Head Station under Captain Kelly and has been connected with this station but one year. Surfman Bangs from his experience as a coastwise sailor, fisherman, and boatman found no difficulty in passing the rigid examination necessary to enter the service, and is a skilled and intrepid life saver.

The No. 6 surfman is Martin Nelson. Surfman Nelson was born in Sweden in 1869. He went to sea when about fifteen years of age and sailed over a great part of the world before he reached the shores of Cape Cod. He has been in the service four years, being assigned to the Monomoy Station under the late Captain Tuttle when he entered the service. Surfman Nelson was also a member of the crew of the Monomoy Station under the late Captain Eldredge, being transferred to the Race Point Station but a short time before. Captain Eldredge and all but one of his boat's crew lost their lives. Surfman Nelson came of a seafaring family and seems especially fitted for the hard life that he has chosen. He married Louise C. Smith, of Provincetown, and is the father of a boy.

The No. 7 surfman is Eugene R. Conwell. He was born in Provincetown in 1880, and is the youngest member of the crew of this station. Surfman Conwell entered the service in June, 1902, being stationed on the floating station at City Point during the summer season, coming to this station in December, 1902. Surfman Conwell, while a young man, is an experienced boatman and has the youth and vigor that will help to make him a valuable member of any life-saving crew to which he may become attached.

HIGH HEAD STATION.

This station was established and manned in 1883 by Captain Kelley and a crew of trained surfmen. The station is three and one-half miles northwest of Cape Cod Highland Light, and its approximate position as obtained from the lastest coast survey charts is latitude 42° 03' 55", longitude west 70° 06' 50". From Provincetown the station is about five miles distant. The eastern end of the dreaded

Peaked Hill Bars extend along the coast at this station, and from wrecks that have taken place on these bars the crew of the station have made many daring rescues. The surfmen at this station exchange checks with the surfmen from the Highland Station on the east and the Peaked Hill Bars Station on the west.

The patrol is about one and one-half miles each way, the shortest patrol on the entire coast of Cape Cod. The station is supplied with two surf-boats, a practice-boat, three beach carts with guns, breeches-buoys, etc., and a life-car.

The practice-boat came from the Peaked Hill Bars Station, and is the one which was capsized at the wreck of the schooner *C. M. Trum-*

HIGH HEAD STATION.

bull at the time the late Captain Atkins, keeper of the Peaked Hill Bars Station, and two members of his crew lost their lives. A surf-boat and beach cart are kept in a house near the beach to be near at hand in the event of disaster. The horse kept at the station is owned by Captain Kelley, and is employed by the government during the winter season, to help drag the apparatus at the time of a wreck.

Capt. Charles P. Kelley, keeper of the High Head Station, with his crew of life savers, have taken thirty-seven persons ashore in their surf-boat during the twenty years that Captain Kelley has been in charge. The breeches-buoy has not been used in active service within the patrol of the station, however, since Captain Kelley assumed command. From the schooner *Laura Brown* five men were rescued and the vessel saved; from the brig *Emily T. Sheldon* eight men were taken ashore, the vessel becoming a total loss. The schooner *Oliver Ames*, which stranded near the station, was saved with her crew of seven.

From the schooner *Plymouth Rock*, which became a total wreck near the station, the crew of six were saved. The crew of the *Abbie H. Hodgman*, five in number, were saved and the vessel floated. The sloop *Red Rover*, which was a total wreck, had her crew of two men rescued. The schooner *Lucia Porter*, with a crew of six men, were saved by the crew of this station, as was the schooner *William H. Oler* and her crew, eight in number.

From the schooner *Jennie C. May* three persons were taken ashore,

HANNAH E. SHEWBERT.

the vessel finally becoming a total loss. The schooner *Carrie Richardson* had her crew of four men taken off by the life savers, the vessel becoming a total wreck, and from the schooner *Job H. Jackson*, which, also, became a total wreck, the life savers, under Captain Kelley, rescued the crew of four men.

CAPT. CHARLES P. KELLEY.

Capt. Charles P. Kelley, keeper of the High Head Life-Saving Station, was born in the village of South Yarmouth, Mass., in the year 1850.

He attended the public schools in his native village until he was a young man, when he went to sea. His first experience being on a fishing vessel. Later he engaged in the coastwise service, and after a number of years joined the fleet of merchantmen which, at that time, carried on an extensive trade with the West Indies.

At the age of twenty-nine, Captain Kelley left the merchant service and joined the crew of life savers under the late Capt. David H. Atkins, at the Peaked Hill Bars Life-Saving Station.

Captain Kelley was attached to the Peaked Hill Bars Station for

CAPT. CHARLES P. KELLEY, KEEPER OF HIGH HEAD.

about three years, during which time he had a number of thrilling experiences and narrow escapes from death in the performance of his duty.

At the time of the wreck of the sloop *C. M. Trumbull*, on Peaked Hill Bars, Captain Kelley was in the life-boat with Captain Atkins going off to the rescue of the imperiled crew, when the latter and two members of the crew lost their lives.

It was Captain Kelley who discovered the sloop stranded on the bars. The life-boat was quickly manned and put off to the wrecked vessel, and in a short time three of the crew were landed on the beach. A second trip through the breakers was safely made, and the boat was alongside the sloop, ready to take off the remaining two members, when the boom of the sloop caught the life-boat under the belt, and capsized it, throwing all hands into the boiling sea.

The night was intensely dark and the weather freezing cold. Captain Atkins was never seen, and the other two members of the boat's crew perished after repeated attempts to get into their boat.

Captain Kelley, surfman as he was then, together with "Sam" Fisher, now keeper of the Race Point Station, and Isaiah H. Young reached the shore after a terrible struggle, and were pulled out of the surf by the members of the crew who had remained ashore.

All three were more dead than alive. The bodies of Captain Atkins and the two members of the crew, Elisha Taylor and Frank A. Mayo, were afterwards found on the beach by the life savers of an adjoining station.

Captain Kelley had been in the service but about a year when he passed through this terrible experience, yet he remained at the dangerous Peaked Hill Bars Station for three years under the late Capt. Isaac G. Fisher, being transferred to the High Head Station as keeper when the station was first manned in 1883.

Captain Kelley had such a wide and varied experience when following the sea, and later as a surfman attached to the Peaked Hill Bars Station, that he was especially well qualified for the responsible position of keeper of the High Head Station, where he has been in command for over twenty years.

During his long term of service as keeper he has been called upon at times to face the elements when they were in their greatest fury, yet he has unflinchingly responded to every call, and, with the surfmen under his charge, have had many thrilling experiences, and endured untold hardship. Captain Kelley was twice married; his present wife was Hannah C. Graham. He is the father of one child, a daughter.

HIGH HEAD STATION CREW.

The No. 1 surfman is Fred C. Franzer. He was born in Provincetown, Aug. 19, 1863, and has been a member of the crew of this station for sixteen years, or ever since he joined the service. He had been a boatman, fisherman, coastwise sailor, and whaleman before entering the service. He is a most experienced life saver, an expert surfman, and a faithful coast guardian. He married Catherine Sylvey, of Provincetown.

The No. 2 surfman is Benjamin Kelley. He was born in West Dennis, and is forty-eight years of age. He went to sea at an early age and made a number of voyages to the Atlantic whaling grounds, and until he joined the service, sixteen years ago, had followed the sea in one capacity or another. Surfman Kelley is at present on sick leave, suffering from injuries received in the performance of duty, his place at the station being filled by his son. Until he received the injuries which compelled him to retire temporarily from the service, he had

A. A. BAKER.　　　H. H. KELLEY.　DAVID B. SNOW.　　　ROB'T E. ELLIS.
　　　L. C. MULLET.　　CAPTAIN KELLEY.　CURTIS F. HIGGINS.
HIGH HEAD CREW.

faithfully performed the arduous duties of the life of a surfman, and was an efficient and trustworthy life saver. He married Susan C. Snow, and is the father of two children, a son and daughter.

The No. 3 surfman is Robert E. Ellis. He was born in Woburn, Mass., is thirty-four years of age, and has been a member of this crew for three years. He was a boatman and fisherman before entering the service, and under the instruction of Captain Kelley has made an able and fearless life saver.

The No. 4 surfman is Albert A. Baker. He was born in Chatham, and is thirty-four years of age. Surfman Baker has been in the service four years, joining this station when he entered. He was a coastwise sailor, boatman, and fisherman before entering the service, and has made an efficient and faithful life saver. He married Susie A. Pratt, and is the father of three boys.

The No. 5 surfman is David B. Snow. He was born in Wellfleet, is twenty-five years of age, and has been in the service two years. He followed the sea from the time he was fourteen years of age until he entered the life-saving service. He is a skilful boatman and an efficient life saver.

The No. 6 surfman is Curtis F. Higgins. He was born in Orleans, and is thirty-two years of age. He has been a member of this crew for two years, entering the service after following the sea as a boatman, yachtsman, towboatman, and a steamshipman. From his experience in the different kinds of work on the water in which he had engaged, he was well prepared for the work of a surfman, and has made an able and faithful life saver. He married Leonora B. Jason.

The No. 7 surfman is Samuel C. Mullett. He was born in Chatham, and is thirty-four years of age. Surfman Mullett is the winter man at this station, joining the station in December and remaining until May following. He has been in the service for three years. During the summer seasons he is a member of the City Point Station, South Boston. Surfman Mullett followed the sea from the time that he was a boy until he entered the service. He is an experienced surfman and well fitted for the hardships that he is called upon to endure as a life saver. He married Mrs. Bessie Cash.

WOOD END STATION.

This station is one of the new type of life-saving stations, with commodious quarters for the keeper and crew, large boat room and lookout. It was built in 1896, and manned in 1897. The late Capt. Isaac G. Fisher, who was keeper of the Peaked Hill Bars Station at the time, was placed in charge of the station and a picked crew of surfmen. Captain Fisher continued as keeper until ill-health caused him to resign from the service. Capt. William Sparrow, now keeper of the Point Allerton Station, who was No. 1 man under Captain Fisher, acted as temporary keeper until Captain Bickers was placed in charge. The station is located on the narrow strip of beach at the tip end of Cape Cod, Provincetown, one-eighth of a mile east from the Wood End lighthouse. Its approximate position as obtained from the latest coast survey charts is latitude north 42° 01' 15", longitude west 70° 11' 30". From Provincetown the distance to the station over the sand dunes and along the beach is about three and one-half miles. Across the head of the harbor, a way that is accessible when the tide has ebbed, the distance is much shorter. The station is supplied with two five-oared surf-boats of the Race Point model, two beach carts, with guns, breeches-buoys, etc., and one life-car. The patrol from this station extends three and three-quarters miles north, and two and one-quarter miles south. This is the only station on Cape Cod where the surfmen do not meet and exchange checks with the surfmen from other stations, time clocks being employed to record the performance of duty of the patrol.

No total wrecks have occurred within the province of this station since Captain Bickers has been in command, and no persons have been taken ashore by the crew either in the surf-boat or breeches-

WOOD END STATION.

buoy, although a large number of vessels have met with disaster near there. The following vessels have been assisted and floated by Captain Bickers and crew: the yawl *Adventurer*, the barge *Paxnos*, and the schooners *Clara*, *Zephyr*, *Caviar*, *Manomet*, *Joseph I. Johnson*, *St. Bernard*, *Marjorie Brown*, *Gladstone*, and *Lewis H. Giles*. Captain Bickers and his crew also assisted in the rescue of the two men, members of the crew of the schooner *Two Forty*, who had been adrift in an open boat for fourteen hours.

"Tom," the pet cat at the Wood End Station, while not being able to aid in the work of life saving, often goes out with the surfmen on their lonely patrol along the beaches to keep them company. "Tom" knows every foot of the beaches and seems to delight in going out with the surfmen, whether the weather is fair or stormy. "Tom" often meets the surfmen half-way along the beach as they are returning from their patrol, running along ahead of the men as if to show them the way to the station. "Tom" is the pet of the crew and is well taken care of by them.

"Jim," the horse which is at the Wood End Station, is owned by Captain Bickers, the keeper. He was raised on Cape Cod, and has been connected with the station for one year or since Captain Bickers assumed charge of the station. "Jim" is an intelligent animal, and has upon more than one occasion been of valuable service to the crew, by

JIM, THE HORSE KEPT AT WOOD END STATION.

hauling apparatus to scenes of disaster. "Jim" knows when bad weather prevails, and is ever ready to do his share in the work of saving life or property.

CAPT. GEORGE H. BICKERS.

Capt. George H. Bickers, keeper of the Wood End Life-Saving Station, was born in Charlestown, Mass., in 1858. He has been in the life-saving service for eleven years, ten as a surfman at Race Point and one as keeper of the Wood End Station. After leaving school, when a young boy, Captain Bickers shipped before the mast on a coasting schooner. He followed coasting for a few years, when he went whaling. As a whaleman he learned the art of handling boats in riotous waters as well as seamanship in all its branches. Captain Bickers followed the sea until he was thirty-three years of age, when he entered the life-saving service, being assigned to the Race Point Station under Capt. "Sam" Fisher. From his experience as a sailor and whaleman he was well fitted for the duties of a life saver. He remained a member of the Race Point crew until the death of Capt. Isaac G. Fisher, keeper of the Wood End Station, when he was appointed to fill the vacancy. Captain Bickers enjoyed an enviable record as a surfman, and has made a record since being keeper of the Wood End Station that places him in the front rank of life savers. One disaster followed another near his station soon after he assumed

CAPT. GEORGE H. BICKERS, KEEPER OF WOOD END STATION.

command, yet not a life was lost, and nearly every craft was saved from destruction by his brave and vigilant crew. But one mishap has occurred since Captain Bickers took charge of the station, the capsizing of the surf-boat while going to a wrecked fishing vessel. The crew quickly righted their boat, bailed her out, went to the wreck, and saved the craft from destruction. Captain Bickers has a crew of skilled and fearless life savers who are ever ready to obey his commands.

He married Abbie L. Cahoon, and is the father of a son.

WOOD END STATION CREW.

The No. 1 surfman is Francesco A. Silva. He was born in Fayal, Azore Islands, in 1863, and has been in the life-saving service for six years, all of which have been spent at this station. Surfman Silva went to sea when a boy, sailing before the mast on a merchant ship. Later he became a whaleman, voyaging from one part of the world to the other in pursuit of the monsters of the deep. Surfman Silva per-

CAPTAIN BICKERS. JONATHAN C. SMALL. ALBERT G. MABBETT. JAMES E. WORTH.
FRANCESCO A. SILVA. FRANK C. WAGES. WILLIE F. ELDREDGE.
WOOD END CREW.

formed his first work as a life saver under the late Capt. Isaac G. Fisher, and soon became an experienced and efficient surfman. He married Julia A. Lornes, and is the father of a son.

The No. 2 surfman is Jonathan C. Small. He was born in Provincetown, and is twenty-six years of age. Surfman Small engaged in boating and fishing off the shores of Cape Cod from the time he was a boy until he entered the life-saving service, and was well fitted for the position he now holds. He has been in the service five years, and is an experienced and fearless life saver.

The No. 3 surfman is Frank C. Wages. He was born in Province-town in 1869, and has been in the life-saving service at this station since it was manned in 1897. Surfman Wages was a sailor and fisherman along the shores of Cape Cod before entering the service, and has made an able and faithful life saver. He married Phœbe Silva, and is the father of a son.

The No. 4 surfman is Albert G. Mabbett. He was born in Whitehall, N. Y., in 1872, and has been in the life-saving service for six years. He shipped as a sailor before the mast on a coasting vessel when he was a boy, and spent several years in the coasting trade. Later he made a number of trips on the United States school ship *St. Mary*, going on cruises to England, Ireland, and through the Straits of Gibraltar to the ports along the Mediterranean Sea. Prior to

MARY NASON WRECKED AT WOOD END.

entering the life-saving service as a regular surfman, he had substituted at other stations along the shores of Cape Cod. As a substitute he performed meritorious service, and has made an efficient and brave life saver. He married Grace May Henderson, and is the father of two daughters and a son.

The No. 5 surfman is Willie F. Eldredge. He was born in Chatham, is thirty-six years of age, and has been in the life-saving service three years. Before entering the service he was a boatman and fisherman along the Chatham shores, and from his experience in that work was well prepared for the duties of a surfman. He also substituted at many of the life-saving stations along the shores of Cape Cod, and is an experienced and efficient life saver.

The No. 6 surfman is James E. Worth. He was born in Provincetown in 1861, and has been in the life-saving service one year. When a boy Surfman Worth went cod fishing to the Grand Banks, and later shipped on a merchant vessel and made a great number of trips to the West Indies Islands and South American ports. After a few years in the merchant service he became a whaleman, and in that service had a number of thrilling experiences. After giving up going to sea he became a baggage-master on the Old Colony Railroad. Later he entered the employ of the Cold Storage Plant at Provincetown, remaining there until he entered this service. When he entered the service he was assigned to the Muskeget Station on Nantucket, and was later transferred to this station. He is an expert boatman and a brave and hardy life saver. He married Nellie P. Lewis, and is the father of two daughters and four sons.

The No. 7 surfman is John N. Lewis. He was born in Provincetown, and is thirty-eight years of age. Until he entered the service four years ago, he had followed the sea from a boy. For three years he was a member of the City Point Station, South Boston, during the summer seasons, and also spent one season at the Straitsmouth Station, Cape Ann. Surfman Lewis is a skilled boatman, and has proved that he can be depended upon to do his duty in any emergency.

PAMET RIVER STATION.

The Pamet River Station is another of the original nine stations which were erected on Cape Cod in 1872. It is located three and one-half miles south of Cape Cod Highland Light, its approximate position as obtained from the latest coast survey charts is latitude north 42° 00′ 00″, longitude west 70° 01′ 15″.

The station stands on one of the high sand dunes which line the ocean shore in Truro village about three miles from the Truro railroad station. When the station was built it stood several hundred feet back from high water mark, but the sea has made such great inroads into the sand dunes at that point on the beach, that the high water mark is now less than one hundred feet distant from the station, which will soon have to be moved to insure its safety. Sand bars with but a small depth of water over them fringe the shore at this station, extending seaward for several hundred yards, and the history of the station records many fearful disasters on them. It was on these dreaded bars that the terrible ocean tragedy, the wreck of the ship *Jason*, occurred, and also where the three crafts, the *Powwow*, *Miles Standish*, and the *E. Pavey*, were wrecked at one time. The wreck of the *Jason* was one of the most appalling disasters that has ever taken place on the shores of Cape Cod, twenty-six lives being lost. Of the whole crew, Samuel Evans, the ship's apprentice, was the only person that managed to reach the shore. Of the whole number, thirty-four, aboard the ships *Powwow*, *Miles Standish*, and *Pavey*, twelve were lost.

The surfmen from this station have a patrol that extends two and one-half miles north and about an equal distance south, the surfmen meeting and exchanging checks on the south patrol with the surfmen from Cahoon's Hollow on the north with the surfmen from the Highland Station.

The patrol is exceedingly hazardous and difficult. When the tide is high the surfmen are driven to the tops of the sand dunes and obliged to grope their way along the crest of the cliffs, which in many places are a hundred feet above the sea-level.

When the station was manned, Capt. Jonathan Lee was appointed

PAMET RIVER STATION.

keeper. He was succeeded by Capt. Nelson W. Weston, George W. Kelley, and Capt. John H. Rich, the latter being succeeded by the present keeper, Capt. George W. Bowley.

Captain Bowley has been in charge of this station but a little over one year, during which time no wrecks have occurred within the territory covered by the patrol from the station, and the crew has been called upon but twice to assist disabled vessels. The first assistance rendered by Captain Bowley after his appointment as keeper was to a big tug boat which got caught on the bars off the shore and was in great peril. The next call was to assist a steam yacht which became disabled off the shore near the station.

This station is supplied with two surf-boats of the Monomoy model, two beach carts with full sets of apparatus, and one life-car. "Johnny," a horse owned by Captain Bowley, is employed by the government during the winter season to assist in hauling the apparatus to wrecks.

CAPT. GEORGE W. BOWLEY.

Capt. George W. Bowley, keeper of the Pamet River Life-Saving Station, was born in Provincetown, Sept. 27, 1870, and has been in

CAPT. GEORGE W. BOWLEY, KEEPER OF PAMET RIVER STATION.

the United States Life-Saving Service for eleven years, ten as a surfman at the Highland Station at North Truro, and one year as keeper of this station.

Captain Bowley came from a family of life savers, his father having been a surfman at the High Head Station, in Provincetown, for

The Life Savers of Cape Cod.

eighteen years, being forced to resign on account of ill-health caused by the hardship he had suffered in that long term of service.

Captain Bowley when a boy was employed as a messenger at the telegraph station in his native town. Later he went to sea on a coasting vessel, and afterwards made a number of voyages to the West Indies. He spent a number of years fishing along the shores of Cape Cod, entering the service when he was twenty-one years of age. The training as a life saver which he received at the Highland Station, under the veteran keeper, Captain Worthen, not only made him a No. 1 surfman, but also fitted him for the higher position which he now holds.

Since he has been keeper of the Pamet River Station, Captain Bowley has spared no pains to maintain a high standard of efficiency and discipline, and he has a crew of trained surfmen ever ready to obey his commands.

PAMET RIVER STATION CREW.

The No. 1 surfman is Ephraim S. Dyer. He was born in Truro in 1845, and has the distinction of being the oldest surfman in point of years of service among the life savers of Cape Cod, if not in the United States. He joined the service when it was established on Cape Cod, and has been attached to the Pamet River Station ever since that time. Before entering the service Surfman Dyer went to sea for a number of years, following the coastwise trade. He also spent a number of years as a fisherman and boatman along the shores of Cape Cod, and was in every way qualified for the position he has held for so long a time. During his long term of service Surfman Dyer has had many narrow escapes from death in the performance of his duty. Upon one occasion when three wrecks, the *Powwow*, *Miles Standish*, and *Pavey*, occurred at one time,

SURFMAN E. S. DYER, PAMET RIVER STATION.
Oldest surfman in the United States Life-saving Service.

he became entangled in the wreckage of one of the vessels, and a big rope, becoming twisted around his legs, dragged him to the bottom, nearly drowning him. During the thirty years that he has been connected with this station, Surfman Dyer has assisted at all the wrecks that have occurred near there, and beyond a sprained ankle he has never received any other injury in the work of saving life and property. The hardships which he has suffered in thirty years do not appear to have affected him in the least. He is hale and hearty and ever ready to respond to the call " vessel ashore."

Surfman Dyer was twice married; his present wife was formerly Lydia Moore. He has one child, a daughter.

The No. 2 surfman is Joseph H. Atwood. He was born in Wey-

E. S. DYER.   R. F. HONEY.   G. W. PAINE.   A. NICKERSON.
J. H. ATWOOD.   CAPTAIN BOWLEY.   I. T. HATCH.
PAMET RIVER CREW.

mouth, Mass., in 1845, and has been in the life-saving service for seventeen years, all of which have been spent at this station. Surfman Atwood went to sea when he was but nine years of age.

For thirty-one years he followed the sea in one capacity or another, making a number of voyages to the West Indies, in engaging in the coastwise trade. From his long years of service on the water he was especially adapted for the arduous duties of a surfman. He has had many thrilling experiences as a surfman. Once he had his leg fractured in assisting at a wreck, and later at the wreck of the schooner

Campbell he was hit on the head by a falling spar and nearly killed. He was twice married; his present wife was formerly Mary Dyer. He is the father of two daughters.

The No. 3 surfman is Richard Honey. He was born in Truro in 1862, and has been in the life-saving service for twelve years, all of which have been at this station. Surfman Honey was a sailor before entering the service. He was an expert boatman when a boy, and after entering the service he quickly became familiar with the work incident to a surfman's life, and has made a faithful and fearless life saver. He married Drusilla Gray.

The No. 4 surfman is George Paine. He was born in Truro, and is forty-eight years of age. Surfman Paine has been in the life-saving service and a member of the Pamet River crew for twelve years. When a young man he went to sea on a coasting schooner. Later he became a trap fisherman and was stationed at Sandwich and other points along the bay shore for a number of years.

As a trap fisherman he was obliged to battle with the surf, and he has few equals as a boatman.

He possessed the highest qualifications when he entered the service, and has made a brave and trustworthy life saver. He married Annie Allen, and is the father of five children, three girls and two boys.

The No. 5 surfman is Isaiah T. Hatch. He was born in Truro in 1857. He first entered the life-saving service in 1888, remaining at this station for one year. He reentered the service in 1892, and again became a member of this crew. Surfman Hatch followed the sea as a sailor boatman and fisherman from the time he was a young man until he entered the service, and was familiar with the duties which he has been called upon to perform as a life saver. He is a skilled boatman and a brave and hardy son of Cape Cod, who knows no peril when duty calls. He married Katie Rogers.

The No. 6 surfman is Manuel Cory. He was born in Provincetown in 1869, and has been in the life-saving service for seven years, all of which have been spent at this station. Surfman Cory was a boatman and fisherman before he entered the service. He is a perfect type of a life saver. Of perfect physique and muscles of steel, the rigors and perils of his vocation have no terrors for him. He is skilled in boating and every branch of the work of life saving, a surfman, who knows no fear when duty calls. He married Mabel F. Snow.

The No. 7 surfman is Alonzo Nickerson. He was born in Harwich in 1871, and has been in the service five years. He was a boatman and fisherman before entering the service, and has made a skilled and faithful life-saver.

ORLEANS STATION.

This station is another of the original nine stations erected on the shores of Cape Cod in 1872. It is located on what is called Little Ponchet Island, back of the Nauset Beach, about two and one-half miles south of Nauset Harbor, and about five miles from the Orleans village. Its approximate position, as obtained from the latest coast survey charts, is latitude north 41° 45′ 35″, longitude west 69° 56′ 00″.

The first keeper of the station was the late Captain Solomon Linnell, who was succeeded by Capt. Marcus Pierce. Captain Pierce was keeper of the station for fifteen years, and upon his retiring from the service, Capt. James H. Charles was placed in command.

ORLEANS STATION.

The station is located at one of the most dangerous sections of the coast, sunken bars stretching along the coast there for miles. The patrol north from this station extends as far as Nauset Harbor, two and one-half miles, the surfmen using time clocks. The south patrol covers two and one-half miles of beach, the surfmen meeting and exchanging checks with the surfmen from the Old Harbor Station. Before the Old Harbor Station was built, the surfmen from this station were obliged to cover the entire beach south as far as Chatham Harbor, a distance of five miles.

At this station there are three surf-boats, two beach carts with guns, breeches-buoys, etc., and a torch light, the latter which gives a tremendously powerful light and is of great benefit to the life

The Life Savers of Cape Cod.   103

savers while working at wrecks in the night. Captain Charles has a horse at this station which the government employs during the winter season.

Since Captain Charles has been keeper of the Orleans Station nearly one hundred lives have been saved by his crew from wrecked vessels. From the schooner *Lizzie M. Center* sixteen men were taken ashore in the surf-boat by his crew, the schooner being saved. From the steam launch *Etta* ten men were taken ashore in the surf-boat. Two men were rescued from a dory by the surf-boat, and from the schooner *Ann* three men were saved by the surf-boat and the vessel floated. From the schooner *Lottie L. Haskins* fourteen men were taken ashore

ALONG THE SHORE AT ORLEANS STATION.

in the surf-boat and the vessel saved. Two men were taken ashore from a cat-boat, but the life savers could not save the craft. From the schooner *Walter Miller* the crew of five and one woman were taken ashore in the breeches-buoy and the vessel saved. The schooner *Iva Laffrinier*, with crew of five men, was boarded by the life savers, who took the crew ashore, the vessel becoming a total loss. From the steam launch *Zilpha* three men were saved, and from the schooner *Zenobia* the crew of three men were rescued by the surf-boat, and the latter craft saved. From the sloop *Carrol* three men were taken ashore by the surf-boat and the craft saved. From the cat-boat *Mary C* three men were taken ashore in surf-boat. One man from a dory and one from a small cat-boat were also brought ashore in the surf-boat. From the schooner *John L. Parker*, which became a total loss, the crew of six men were taken off by the breeches-buoy. From the schooner *Elsie M. Smith*, which also became a total loss, sixteen men were taken ashore by the breeches-buoy, while from the steam launch *No Name* two men and a woman and child were taken ashore in the surf-boat.

While Captain Charles and his crew have made many daring

STRANDED ON THE OUTER BAR AT ORLEANS, LATER BECOMING A TOTAL WRECK.

rescues both by surf-boat and breeches-buoy, the hardest and most perilous tasks they have are going offshore to the assistance of distressed vessels. These jobs mean long and hard pulls with the perils multiplied, as after boarding the crafts they are often compelled to work them into port. No matter how far offshore the distressed vessel may be, once she is sighted with colors flying at half-mast, Captain Charles and his crew are off to her assistance. Frequently it happens that the vessels they board, after pulling in the teeth of a gale for hours, are in a sinking condition and the crews exhausted. It is then a race for life to port, and many times have the life savers felt the vessels which they have started to take into port sinking under them, before they had gotten under way.

Captain Charles and his crew have had many narrow escapes in going to the assistance of distressed vessels, and have often suffered untold hardship in the work, but that they are ever ready to battle with the wind or wave is evidenced by the great number of heroic rescues they have made.

CAPT. JAMES H. CHARLES.

Capt. James H. Charles, keeper of the Orleans Station, was born in Dennis in 1857, and has been in the life-saving service for fifteen years, six as a surfman and nine as keeper. His whole term of service has been at the Orleans Station.

His father was a well-known sea captain, and Captain Charles took

CAPT. JAMES H. CHARLES, KEEPER OF ORLEANS STATION.

naturally to the life of a sailor. When a young man his family moved to the far West.

Captain Charles remained in the West but a short time, returning to Cape Cod and engaging in boating and fishing along its shores. Later he joined the fleet of cod fishermen, and went to the Grand Banks as a skipper. After a few years as skipper of a "grand banker," he returned to the West, taking up a government grant of land. He remained in the West but a year, returning to Cape Cod, and again joining the fishing fleet. After several seasons with the fishing fleet, he entered the life-saving service, being assigned to the Orleans Station under Capt. Marcus Pierce. As a surfman, under the veteran Captain Pierce, Captain Charles displayed exceptional ability as a boatman and life saver. The training he received with Captain Pierce soon fitted him for the position to which he was subsequently promoted, keeper of the station, succeeding Captain Pierce. Since he has had charge of the station, a high standard of efficiency has always been maintained, and the daring rescues which the crew of his station has performed testifies to their efficiency, fearlessness, and skill. Captain Charles married Lizzie Hurd, and is the father of three daughters and one son.

ORLEANS STATION CREW.

The No. 1 surfman is Abbott H. Walker. He was born in Orleans, Sept. 25, 1864, and has been in the life-saving service for eight years. Surfman Walker followed the sea from boyhood, and was a well-known boatman and fisherman. He acquired the art of handling boats in the surf when a boy and knows the location of every rip and shoal along the coast of Cape Cod. He had his first experience as a life saver under Captain Charles, and has made a skilled, fearless, and efficient coast guardian. He married Lillie Wiley, and is the father of two daughters and two sons.

The No. 2 surfman is Richard S. Gage. He was born in Dennis in 1858, and has been in the life-saving service for eleven years. Before becoming a regular surfman he substituted at the Monomoy and at this station. When he was appointed a regular surfman he was assigned to the Pamet River Station, where he served for three years. He was a boatman and fisherman for years, and also a coastwise and deep water sailor. Surfman Gage is a perfect type of life saver. Skilled in the art of boating, absolutely fearless, he has made a brave and hardy surfman.

He married Hannah M. Ellis, and is the father of two daughters and two sons.

The No. 3 surfman is Nehemiah P. Hopkins. He was born in Eastham in 1875, and has been in the life-saving service for six years. He spent his boyhood days boating and fishing along the shores of Cape Cod, and had a wide experience on the water before he entered the service. The training he has received at this station has made him a brave and efficient life saver. He married Geneva Eldredge, and is the father of two sons.

The No. 4 surfman is William B. Sherman. He was born in Orleans in 1857, and has been in the life-saving service for seven years. Surfman Sherman was assigned to this station when he entered the service, but resigned after a few months. When he reentered he was sent to the Coskata Station on Nantucket, and was later transferred to this station. He came from a seafaring family, his father having been an old "Grand Banker." Surfman Sherman learned the art of handling boats in the surf before he joined the service, and has made an intrepid and skilled life saver. He married Minnie Cormaney, and is the father of one daughter and three sons.

The No. 5 surfman is Timothy F. Murray. He was born in Boston in 1859, and has been in the life-saving service three years. Before entering the service he had engaged in fishing and steamboating, and was a coastwise sailor and mariner. He was assigned to this station

CAPTAIN CHARLES. RICHARD S. GAGE. WILLIAM B. SHERMAN. JOHN KILBURN.
ABBOTT H. WALKER. NEHEMIAH P. HOPKINS. TIMOTHY F. MURRAY. GEO. F. JORDEN.
ORLEANS STATION CREW.

when he joined the service, and has made an able and skilled life saver. He married Phœbe F. Chase, and is the father of two daughters and one son.

The No. 6 surfman is John Kilburn. He was born in Provincetown in 1856, and has been in the life-saving service for three years. When he entered the service he was assigned to the Gay Head Station on Martha's Vineyard, where he served one year, when he was sent to the Cahoon's Hollow Station, remaining there one year. Surfman Kilburn was a mariner before entering the service, and was well fitted for the work he is called upon to perform as a life saver. He married Eliza Sparrow, and is the father of two sons.

The No. 7 surfman is George F. Jorden. He was born in Williamsport, Pa., in 1875, and has been in the life-saving service for two years. He entered the service as a member of the City Point, South Boston, Station crew. He served there two seasons and was the winterman at Wood End Station under Captain Bickers for two years. Last May he was transferred to the Salisbury Beach Station, where he remained until Dec. 1, 1902, when he joined this station.

Surfman Jorden had substituted at this station before he joined the service. He is an expert boatman and a fearless life saver. He married Sarah Smith, and is the father of one daughter and one son.

NAUSET STATION.

The Nauset Life-Saving Station is another of the original nine United States Life-Saving Stations which were built on Cape Cod in 1872.

NAUSET STATION.

It is situated on Nauset beach about two and one-half miles from North Eastham depot and village. Its approximate position as obtained from the latest coast survey charts is latitude north 41° 50′ 40″, longitude west 69° 45′ 00″. When this station was built it was placed on a site one thousand feet south of its present location, but the shifting sands soon required its being moved inland to a more secure location, the site it now occupies. The sea at this point is constantly making great inroads into the beach, the banks having been cut away for a distance of about one hundred and fifty feet since the station was built.

The patrol north from this station is about four and one-half miles, the surfmen meeting and exchanging checks with the surfmen from Cahoon's Hollow. The south patrol is three and one-eighth miles, the surfmen that go on that patrol using time clocks to record their performance of duty.

Nauset bars extend along the shore at this station, and many terrible wrecks have taken place there. When the station was opened Capt.

SURFMAN WALKER. SURFMAN GAGE. CAPTAIN BEARSE. CAPTAIN CHARLES.
SURFMAN SNOW. SURFMAN JORDEN. SURFMAN HOWES. SURFMAN HIGGINS.

JOINT CREW.

Captains Charles, of Orleans Station, and Bearse, of Nauset Station, with their picked crews of life savers who, at the risk of their lives, brought the disabled schooner *Andrew Adams* and crew into port. This, the first instance in the history of the life-saving service on Cape Cod, in which two life-saving captains went to a rescue in the same life-boat, occurred during the winter of 1903.

Marcus M. Pierce was appointed keeper. Later he was transferred to the Orleans Station, and Capt. Walter D. Knowles was placed in charge. Keeper Knowles was succeeded by the present keeper Captain Bearse. There are two surf-boats of the Monomoy model, two beach carts with breeches-buoy, etc., and a life-car at this station.

"Brad," a horse owned by Captain Bearse, is on duty at the station during the winter season.

Captain Bearse and his crew of life savers have rescued seventeen persons in their surf-boat and seventeen shipwrecked sailors in the breeches-buoy since Captain Bearse has been keeper, while thirty-eight persons were rescued from the surf by ropes and small boats. Of the total number of vessels stranded on the bars near the station eight schooners and one cat-boat were a total loss. Not a life has been lost within the province of this station since Captain Bearse has been in charge.

CAPT. ALONZO N. BEARSE.

Capt. Alonzo N. Bearse, keeper of the Nauset Life-Saving Station, was born on Monomoy Point in 1842, and has been in the life-saving serv-

CAPT. ALONZO N. BEARSE, KEEPER OF NAUSET STATION.

ice for nineteen years, three years as a surfman and sixteen as keeper of this station. Born on Monomoy Island, within sight of the dreaded shoals off Monomoy, as a boy he became familiar with boats and boating, and witnessed the scenes of disaster that occurred along the coast near his home. He quickly learned the art of handling boats in rough water, and in launching and landing through the surf. He went to sea at an early age, shipping on a coastwise schooner. Returning from sea shortly after the outbreak of the Civil War, he enlisted in the 43d Massachusetts Infantry, Company E, serving honorably with his company for eleven months, his term of enlistment. During the time that he was at the front he took part in the severe fighting at Kingston, Whitehall, and Goldsboro. He escaped unhurt, however, and returned to Cape Cod, and again went to sea. He had a wide and varied experience as mariner, fisherman, and boatman, and was well qualified for the work of a surfman when he joined the Nauset Station crew, under Captain Knowles, whom he subsequently succeeded as keeper.

Captain Bearse labors diligently to maintain a high standard of efficiency among his crew, and is a careful and fearless warrior of the sea. Numerous disasters have occurred within the precincts of the Nauset Station since he has been in command, and many have been averted, owing to the vigilance of his surfmen.

He was twice married, his present wife was Cordelia Ellis, and he is the father of three children.

NAUSET STATION CREW.

The No. 1 surfman is Allen T. Gill. He was born in North Eastham in 1857, and has been in the life-saving service for sixteen years, all of which have been spent at this station. Surfman Gill followed the sea and was a boatman and fisherman from the time he was a boy until he joined the service. He has assisted at all the wrecks that have occurred along the Nauset beach during the past sixteen years, and is a fearless and faithful coast guardian. He married Exa E. Lewis, and is the father of a daughter and son.

The No. 2 surfman is Charles C. Daniels. He was born in Gloucester, and is forty years of age. Surfman Daniels has been a member of the Nauset crew for fifteen years, being assigned to this station when he entered the service. He went to sea when a young man as a sailor in the coastwise surface, and was also a boat fisherman for a number of years. He was especially fitted for the work of a surfman, and has made a brave and faithful life saver. He married Mary Cole, and is the father of four daughters and two sons.

The No. 3 surfman is Lewis H. Collins. He was born in North Eastham in 1865, and is serving his fourteenth year as a life saver. Surfman Collins was a fisherman and sailor before he entered the service. In the fourteen years that he has been a member of the Nauset crew he has proven himself a faithful and fearless life saver. While working at a wreck several years ago he suffered severe injuries to his leg and back by the capsizing of the surf-boat that rendered him unfit for service for a long time. He married Eva W. Wiley, and is the father of a boy.

The No. 4 surfman is Whitman F. Howes. He was born in Chatham in 1860, and has been in the life-saving service for ten years. Surfman Howes was a boat fisherman and sailor before entering the service, and was well qualified for the work of a surfman when he became a life saver. He has assisted at all the wrecks along the shore during the past ten years and has proven his worth as a life saver

CAPTAIN BEARSE.   CHAS. C. DANIELS.   WHITMAN F. HOWES.   WARREN F. MAYO.
   ALLEN T. GILL.   LEWIS H. COLLINS.   ORIN W. HIGGINS.   GEORGE F. SNOW.
NAUSET CREW.

whenever duty called him. He married Carrie L. Penniman, and is the father of one daughter and one son.

The No. 5 surfman is Orin W. Higgins. He was born in Eastham in 1867, and has been in the life-saving service for nine years, all of which have been spent at this station. As a sailor and boat fisherman along the shores of Cape Cod, Surfman Higgins was well accustomed to the handling of boats in the roughest water, and has made an able and trustworthy life saver. He married Helen F. Higgins.

The No. 6 surfman is Warren W. Mayo. He was born in Eastham, and is thirty-three years of age. He entered the life-saving service seven years ago, being assigned to this station. Before entering the service he had followed the sea for a number of years, and was skilled in the art of handling boats. He has made a valuable man for Captain Bearse and is a faithful and fearless life saver. He married Marion M. Sparrow, and is the father of a son and daughter.

The No. 7 surfman is George F. Snow. He was born in Orleans in 1859, and has been in the life-saving service for four years. Surfman Snow is the winter man at this station, joining the crew in December, 1902. For two seasons he has been a member of the City Point, South Boston, Life-Saving Station. He was a boatman and fisherman along the shores of the Cape before entering the service, and has made an able and faithful life saver. He married Susan W. Alden, and is the father of one daughter and three sons.

OLD HARBOR STATION.

This station, at the entrance of Chatham Old Harbor, has been in commission less than five years, during which time Keeper Doane and

OLD HARBOR STATION.

his crew have rescued twenty-one persons in their surf-boat and taken thirteen shipwrecked sailors ashore in the breeches-buoy. Of the whole number of vessels that met with disaster within the province of the station, but two were total wrecks, viz., the *Elsie C. Smith* of Gloucester, and the *Commerce* of Rockland, the latter foundering off the shore near the station.

This station is provided with two surf-boats, two beach carts with guns, breeches-buoys, etc., and a life-car. One of the surf-boats, a small one, is kept in a boathouse on the point of the beach, about a half mile from the station, where it can be quickly brought into use for rescue work in the harbor and bay. The other surf-boat, the large one, for use in the open sea, is kept in the station. A horse which the government hires during the winter season is kept in a barn close to the station.

The surfmen from this station have a patrol north for a distance of two and one-half miles, meeting and exchanging checks with the surf-

HEZEKIAH F. DOANE, KEEPER OF OLD HARBOR STATION.

men from the Orleans Station. On the south patrol, which is about a mile, the surfmen use a time clock to register their patrolling of the beach at that point.

CAPT. HEZEKIAH F. DOANE.

Capt. Hezekiah F. Doane, keeper of the Old Harbor Station, was born in Chatham in 1846, and has been in the life-saving service for twenty-two years, thirteen as a surfman and nine as keeper. When he entered the service he was assigned to the Chatham Station, where he served as a surfman for thirteen years, being appointed keeper of the station in 1893. Captain Doane remained keeper of the Chatham Station for five years or until he was transferred to the Old Harbor Station in 1898. He was a fisherman, yachtsman, and mariner before he entered the life-saving service and was well prepared for the work he has since been called upon to perform. As a surfman at the Chatham Station he had much work in rescuing shipwrecked crews and assisting distressed vessels, and his appointment as keeper of the Chatham Station was meritorious reward for faithful and efficient service. While keeper of the Chatham Station, Captain Doane and his brave crew of life savers made many perilous trips out over the shoals to distressed vessels, and effected daring rescues of imperiled crews. Owing to the shallow water along the Chatham shores, nearly all the work performed by Captain Doane was with the surf-boats, the breeches-buoy having been used but twice since he has been in the service. He married Pemah B. Pierce, and is the father of two sons.

OLD HARBOR STATION CREW.

The No. 1 surfman is Robert F. Pierce. He was born in Harwich and is thirty-six years of age. Surfman Pierce has been in the life-saving service for twelve years, eight as a member of the Monomoy crew, under the late Captain Tuttle, and four years at this station. When a young man he engaged in boating and fishing, and later entered the coastwise service. From his experience as a fisherman and boatman along the shores of Cape Cod he was skilled in the art of handling boats in the surf, and took naturally to the work he has been called upon to perform since joining the life-saving service. While a member of the Monomoy crew he was repeatedly called upon to face the greatest dangers, and won for himself an enviable record as a life saver. Surfman Pierce was out of the service one year, during which time he was engaged in boating. He married Minnie A. Bearse, and is the father of a boy.

The No. 2 surfman is Edwin P. Ellis. He was born in Brewster and is forty-five years of age. Surfman Ellis has been in the life-saving service for twelve years. He was a boatman and fisherman before he joined the service. When he entered the service he was assigned to the Orleans Station, under Captain Charles, serving there for five years, when he was transferred to Coskata Station on Nantucket. He was a member of the Coskata Station crew for two years. At the end of that time he was sent to join the crew at this station. At the Orleans and Coskata stations Surfman Ellis received a thorough drilling and performed much active work in life saving. He is a skilful boatman, hardened to the rigors of a life saver's life.

The No. 3 surfman is Benjamin O. Eldredge. He was born in Chatham, on July 10, 1878, and has been in the life-saving service for five years. Prior to his becoming a regular member of this station crew, he served as a substitute at the Monomoy Station, under the late Captains Tuttle and Eldredge. As a boatman and fisherman along the Chatham shore and a substitute life saver he acquired a thorough knowledge of the art of handling boats in the surf under the

CAPTAIN DOANE.   EDWIN P. ELLIS.   OTIS C. ELDREDGE.   ZEBINA B. CHASE.
ROB'T F. PIERCE.   BENJ. O. ELDREDGE.   FRANCIS H. BASSETT.
OLD HARBOR STATION CREW.

most trying conditions, and was well qualified for the duties he has to perform as a life saver.

The No. 4 surfman is Otis C. Eldredge. He was born in Chatham in 1856, and has been in the life-saving service for seven years. When he entered the service he was assigned to the Jerry's Point Station, N. H., under Capt. Silas Harding, remaining there three years, when he was transferred to this station. Before entering the service, Surfman Eldredge was a boat fisherman and "beach comber" along the Chatham shores, and his experience in the work especially fitted him for the duties of a life saver. He married Margaret Bloomer, and is the father of two daughters.

The No. 5 surfman is Dean W. Eldredge. He was born in Brewster, and is forty-seven years of age. Surfman Eldredge has been in the life-saving service for three years. Before entering the service he was a member of the crew of the Handkerchief Lightship. For years he engaged in boating, fishing, and wrecking along the shores of Cape Cod, and is a skilled surfman and a faithful life saver. When he entered the service he was assigned to the Plum Island Station, remaining there but a short time before he was sent to the Orleans Station, from which he was transferred to this station in August, 1902. He married Lena Hallet.

The No. 6 surfman is Francis H. Bassett. He was born in Harwich in 1863, and has been in the life-saving service for three years. He served two years at the Cahoon's Hollow Station, under Captain Cole, becoming a member of this station Dec. 1, 1901. Surfman Bassett was a boatman and fisherman on Chatham bars for a number of years and had also been a grocery man. He had a wide experience as a boatman, and has made an able and fearless life saver. He married Gertrude G. Allen, and is the father of five daughters.

The No. 7 surfman is Zebina B. Chase. He was born in Chatham in 1862, and has been in the life-saving service three years. He was first a member of the Salisbury Beach Station, where he remained one and one-half years, then joining the Floating Station at City Point, South Boston. Before entering the service as a regular surfman he had substituted at different periods for four years at the Monomoy Station. Prior to this he was a member of the crew of the Shovelful Lightship for five years. From the time that he was a boy he has been engaged in boating, or fishing, or doing service of one kind or another on the water along the shores of Cape Cod. He is the winter man at this station, joining the City Point Station crew in the summer season. He is a skilful boatman and an efficient life saver. He married Etta M. Nickerson, and is the father of one daughter and four sons.

CHATHAM STATION.

The Chatham Station is another of the original nine stations erected on Cape Cod in 1872, and is situated near where it was first located. Its approximate position as obtained from the latest coast survey charts is latitude north 41° 39' 10", longitude west 69° 57' 10", one and one-quarter miles southwest of Chatham lights. A few years after the station was established it was moved across the harbor to where the Old Harbor Station now stands. It remained there a few years when it was again moved back to its original site, where it is now located, on the northern end of Monomoy, near the "cut through," within easy distance of Chatham village.

When this station was moved from the Old Harbor site it was believed that a new station would be built there, but not until after the wreck of the schooner *Calvin B. Orcutt* on Old Harbor bars was the station erected. The first keeper of the station was Capt. Alpheus Mayo; he was in turn succeeded by Capt. Nathaniel Gould, Capt. Hezekiah Doane, and the present keeper, Capt. Herbert Eldredge.

The patrol, south from this station, is two and one-quarter miles; the north patrol about two miles. Checks are exchanged with the surfmen from the Monomoy Station on the south; on the north patrol time clocks are used. The station is supplied with four surf-boats, (Monomoy model), one dory, two beach carts with full sets of appa-

CHATHAM STATION.

ratus, and one life-car. "Baby," a horse employed by the government, is kept at the station to assist in hauling the apparatus to wrecks.

WRECKS AT THE CHATHAM STATION.

Since Keeper Eldredge has had charge of this station he has made twenty-six trips to disabled or wrecked vessels in the station surf-boat. On board the vessels assisted by Keeper Eldredge and his crew there were seventy-four persons. Of this number eight were taken ashore in the surf-boat. Six of these comprised the crew of the schooner *Electa Bailey*, which was a total loss, one was from a crippled cat-boat, and the other was a sick sailor taken ashore from a schooner. Most of the work done by the crew of the Chatham Station was on two and three masted schooners that became stranded on the Chatham bars.

CAPT. HERBERT E. ELDREDGE.

Capt. Herbert E. Eldredge, keeper of the Chatham Station, was born in Chatham in 1863, and has been in the life-saving service for thirteen years, eight as a surfman and five as keeper, all of which have been spent at this station. Captain Eldredge began his career on the water along the Chatham shore when a boy of thirteen years, and was an expert boatman, fisherman, and wrecker before he was twenty years

CAPT. HERBERT ELDREDGE, KEEPER OF CHATHAM STATION.

of age. For six years he went fishing on the rips off Chatham, one of the most perilous occupations along the coast. As a member of Capt. Joseph Bloomer's wrecking crew, Captain Eldredge had a wide experience working on wrecked vessels along the coast, and was especially fitted for the responsible position that he now holds. He has a crew of brave and hardy life savers for whom the rips and shoals that abound along the Chatham shore have no terrors. Not a life has been lost within the province of the Chatham Station during the time that Captain Eldredge has been keeper.

He married Mary A. Nye, and is the father of two daughters and a son.

CHATHAM STATION CREW.

The No. 1 surfman is Bradford N. Bloomer. He was born in Chatham in 1871, and has been in the life-saving service for six years, all of which have been spent at this station. Before entering the service Surfman Bloomer was a Monomoy fisherman, so called. In this work he became skilled in the art of handling boats in the surf, and

HERBERT P. SMITH.   JOHN W. CROWELL.   CHARLES H. HOWES.   CAPTAIN ELDREDGE.
NATHANIEL HAMILTON.   SAMUEL D. ELDREDGE.   BRADFORD D. BLOOMER.

CHATHAM CREW.

obtained a knowledge of the shoals that lie hidden along the coast off Chatham that especially fitted him for the work of a surfman. He married Julia Pitts, and is the father of two daughters.

The No. 2 surfman is Charles H. Howes. He was born in Chatham, is thirty-six years of age, and has been in the life-saving service five years. Surfman Howes was assigned to the Coskata Station on Nantucket when he entered the service; later he was transferred here. He was a boatman and fisherman over the Old Harbor bars from boyhood until he entered the life-saving service. The experience he gained in that hazardous work fully prepared him for the duties of a surfman, and he has made a brave and trustworthy life saver. He married Henrietta Jones, and is the father of a daughter and son.

The No. 3 surfman is Samuel D. Eldredge. Surfman Eldredge was born in East Harwich in 1859, and has been in the life-saving service for five years, all of that time at this station. He was a boatman and fisherman from the time that he was a boy until he entered the service, and was in every way qualified for the work of a life saver. He married Sarah J. Eldredge.

The No. 4 surfman is John W. Crowell. He was born in East Harwich, and is twenty-six years of age. Surfman Crowell has been in the life-saving service six years, serving four years at the Monomoy Station under the late Captain Eldredge, the remaining time at this station. Before entering the service he was a boatman and fisherman on the Chatham bars. As a member of the Monomoy crew he was called upon to face the greatest perils in the work of rescuing lives from wrecked vessels, and proved a faithful and brave surfman. He married Elsie Nickerson, and is the father of a son.

The No. 5 surfman is Nathaniel Hamilton. He was born in Foxboro, Mass., in 1872, and has been in the life-saving service for four years. Surfman Hamilton was formerly a member of the Coskata Station, Nantucket. Owing to injuries received by falling on a piece of wreckage, while on patrol duty at that station, he was on sick leave for one year. When he reentered the service he was assigned to this station. He was a boatman and fisherman before entering the service, and has made a brave and efficient life saver. He married Abbie L. Johnson, and is the father of three daughters.

The No. 6 surfman is Franklin W. Eldredge. He was born in Chatham in 1859, and has been in the life-saving service one year. Surfman Eldredge joined the Coskata Station crew when he entered the service, and after five months at that station was transferred here. He was a boatman and fisherman before he entered the service, spending thirteen years as a fisherman over Chatham bars. He entered the life-saving service fully prepared for the most perilous work, and has proved to be a skilled and faithful life saver. He married Modena B. Jerauld, and is the father of three daughters and two sons.

The No. 7 surfman is Herbert P. Smith. He was born in Edgartown, Martha's Vineyard, in 1877, and has been in the life-saving service five years. Surfman Smith was a boatman and fisherman along the shores of Martha's Vineyard from boyhood. In addition to being an expert boatman, he received a thorough nautical training, having made several foreign cruises as a cadet on the United States training ship *Enterprise*. Surfman Smith also served on the repair ship *Vulcan* during the war with Spain.

He is skilled in the art of boating through the surf and has made a faithful and fearless life saver.

MONOMOY STATION.

The Monomoy Station is another of the original nine stations erected on Cape Cod when the United States Life-Saving Service was extended to these shores. It is located two and one-half miles north of Monomoy Light. Its approximate position as obtained from the latest coast survey charts is latitude north 41° 35′ 25″, longitude west 69° 59′ 10″. When the station was manned, March 20, 1873, Capt. George W. Baxter, of West Harwich, was placed in command. He resigned on account of ill-health in 1882, and his successor was Capt. William Tuttle. His death occurred July 1, 1899, and the late Capt. Marshall W. Eldredge was appointed to fill the vacancy Aug. 4, 1899.

MONOMOY STATION.

Captain Eldredge perished in an attempt to rescue five persons from the stranded barge *Wadena*, March 17, 1902.

The patrol north of this station is about two and one-half miles, the surfmen meeting and exchanging checks with the surfmen from the Chatham Station. The patrol south is about one and one-half miles, the surfmen meeting and exchanging checks with the surfmen from the Monomoy Point Station.

There is no more dangerous stretch of coast on Cape Cod than off Monomoy. Disaster follows disaster in that region, and the work of the life savers is attended with the greatest peril at all times.

The following disasters have occurred at the Monomoy Station since Captain Ellis has been in command: Schooner *Elwood Burton*, of New York, stranded on the Handkerchief Shoal, the life savers rescuing her crew of six men in their surf-boat. Five men, the crew of the barge *Paxinos*, which had struck on Pollock Rip, were rescued from a sinking boat by the Monomoy crew. They were later placed aboard the barge, which was soon floated by the life savers. From the schooner *Dora Mathews*, which stranded on the beach near the station,

CAPT. SETH L. ELLIS, KEEPER OF MONOMOY STATION.

three men were taken ashore in the breeches-buoy. A number of other crafts which met with disaster along the shore were assisted by Captain Ellis and his crew.

CAPT. SETH L. ELLIS.

Capt. Seth L. Ellis, keeper of the Monomoy Station and sole survivor of the Monomoy disaster, was born in Harwich Port, Oct. 12, 1858, and has been in the life-saving service seven years, all of which have been at this station.

Captain Ellis came from a family of seafaring people. His father, Capt. Seth N. Ellis, was an old West Indies tradesman.

Captain Ellis went to sea with his father when but nine years of age. When fifteen years of age Captain Ellis joined the fleet of mackerel fishermen, remaining with the fleet until he went coasting. While a member of the crew of the three-masted schooner *Enos B. Phillips*, of Boston, Capt. T. Reuben Allen, of Harwich Port, master, the vessel was struck by a blizzard that made her a helpless wreck. With her jibboom, bowsprit, foremast, and maintop masts gone, all her head sails lost, and the cabin and forecastle wrecked, the schooner was blown across the gulf stream and out of the track of all shipping. After many days, during which the crew suffered terribly, Captain Allen finally triumphed and brought the vessel into port.

Captain Ellis has been master of sailing and steam vessels, and now carries a captain's first-class steamboat license for the Atlantic coast. Captain Ellis was also a well-known mackerel fisherman, being a member of the crew of the first steam fishing vessel employed in mackerel fishery, the *Novelty*, of Boston. Later Captain Ellis engaged in boat fishing along the shores of the Cape near Chatham, continuing in that work until he joined the Monomoy crew of life savers.

MONOMOY STATION CREW.

The No. 1 surfman is Walter C. Bloomer. He was born in Chatham in 1867, and has been in the life-saving service for five years. Surfman Bloomer was a "Monomoy" fisherman, boatman, and wrecker before entering the service. When he joined the service he was assigned to the Brant Rock Station, where he remained three years, being transferred to this station. At this station, under the late Captain Eldredge, he saw much active service and proved himself a fearless and skilful surfman. On the occasion of the terrible Monomoy disaster, when his keeper and six of his comrades lost their lives, Surfman Bloomer was doing cook duty, and remained at the station. He married Velma Stevens, and is the father of two girls and two boys.

The No. 2 surfman is Thomas H. Kane. He was born in Manchester, N. H., in 1870, and has been in the life-saving service four years. Surfman Kane followed the sea from the time he was fifteen years of age until he entered the life-saving service. He was a "grand banker," a mackerel fisherman, and had a wide and varied experience on the water. He was a member of the Rockport Life-Saving crew, and was with Captain Charles at the Orleans Station for one year. Surfman Kane joined the Monomoy Station, to fill a vacancy caused by the death of one of the crew who perished with Captain Eldredge at the Monomoy disaster.

He is an expert boatman, a brave and hardy surfman. He married Sarah Whellock, and is the father of a daughter and son.

The No. 3 surfman is Edwin A. Studley. He was born in North Harwich in 1864, and has been in the life-saving service for two years, one year at the Orleans Station and one year at this station. Surfman Studley followed the sea since he was a boy. For several years he was a member of the crew of the Pollock Rip Lightship, and later he joined the crew of the Shovelful Lightship. He was also a sailor in the coastwise trade, and engaged in boating and fishing along the Chatham shores for several years. He is an efficient boat-

GEORGE CAHOON.   WALTER F. WIXON.
THOMAS H. KANE. WALTER BLOOMER. CAPTAIN ELLIS. SURFMAN RESIGNED. EDWIN A. STUDLEY.
MONOMOY CREW.

man and a fearless life saver. He married Alice Phillips, and is the father of a son.

The No. 4 surfman is George C. Cahoon. He was born in Harwich in 1872, and has been in the life-saving service but a year. When he entered the service he was assigned to the Race Point Station, under Capt. "Sam" Fisher, and was transferred here this year. Surfman Cahoon was a fisherman and boatman along the shores of Cape Cod from the time he was a boy until he entered the service. He is an able boatman and has already shown himself to be an efficient life saver. He married Emma Jones, and is the father of a daughter.

The No. 5 surfman is Walter F. Wixon. He was born in South

Chatham in 1866, and is serving his first year in the life-saving service. Having been a boatman and fisherman along the shores "back of the Cape" for a number of years, he is skilled in handling a boat, and has a thorough knowledge of the rips and shoals that line the shore there. He married Minnie E. Chase.

The No. 6 surfman is Thomas W. Bearse. He was born in West Harwich in 1863, and is serving his first season as a life saver. Surfman Bearse was a boatman and fisherman along the Chatham shores before he entered the service, and was well prepared for the work he has been called upon to perform as a surfman. He married Annie Cahoon, and is the father of two boys.

The No. 7 surfman is Frank Thomas. He was born in Provincetown in 1874, and entered the life-saving service Dec. 1, 1902. Surfman Thomas went to the Grand Banks when he was but eleven years of age. He followed the sea from that time until he entered the service, engaging principally in dory fishing off Cape Cod. He is an expert boatman and gives promise of becoming an able life saver. He married Rosie Gracie, and is the father of two daughters.

The No. 8 surfman is Marcus N. Smith. He was born in West Chatham in 1865, and has been in the life-saving service one year. He followed the sea and was a boatman and fisherman along the shores of Cape Cod from the time he was a boy until he joined the service. He first served at the Muskeget Station, Nantucket, joining this station as the winter man Dec. 1, 1902. He has proved his efficiency as a life saver, and is a valuable addition to the crew at this station.

Owing to the great amount of work which the crew of this station was called upon to perform, and the long patrol that the surfmen were obliged to go over before the Monomoy Point Station was built, eight surfmen were employed at this station, and they are still retained. It is the only station on Cape Cod where that number of surfmen are employed.

MONOMOY POINT STATION.

The Monomoy Point Station is located near the extreme end of Monomoy Island, about nine miles from Chatham lights, which bear about north-northeast. Monomoy Island is a long, narrow strip of beach at the elbow of Cape Cod. The dreaded Shovelful and Handkerchief shoals stretch out under the waters of Nantucket Sound along the eastern and southern shores of the island, and in the vicinity countless vessels have met their doom and many lives have been lost. Owing to the great number of disasters that occurred off the southern end of Monomoy, the present life-saving station was built. At the time that this station was erected it was intended that the old Monomoy Station should be abandoned and the crew transferred to this station.

After the appalling calamity, "The Monomoy Disaster" on March 17, 1902, when Captain Eldredge and six of his crew of life savers lost their lives, the department decided to continue the old Monomoy Station.

The station is one of the most modern buildings of its kind, with large and airy rooms for the crew and a big boat room for the surf-boats, beach carts, and other apparatus.

The patrol north from this station is about one and one-half miles, the surfmen meeting and exchanging checks with the surfmen from

MONOMOY POINT STATION.

the Old Monomoy Station. The south patrol along the beach on the end of Monomoy is also about one and one-half miles, the surfman on that patrol carrying a time clock to record their performance of duty.

At the Monomoy Point Station there are three surf-boats. One of these boats is a self-bailer, the only one on Cape Cod. There are also two beach carts with apparatus, and one life-car. Six surfmen with Keeper Kelley go in the self-bailer at the time of shipwreck. A horse owned by the government, called "Susan," is kept at the station to assist in hauling the apparatus to scenes of disaster. There are also two other horses owned by the surfmen kept there. Cats are the pets of the surfmen, a half dozen making their home at the station.

CAPT. JOSEPH C. KELLEY.

Capt. Joseph C. Kelley, keeper of the Monomoy Point Life-Saving Station, was born in West Brewster in 1873, and has been in the life-saving service for five years. When he entered the service he was assigned to the Peaked Hill Bars Station under Captain Cook. He remained there but a few months, when he was transferred to the Chatham Station under Capt. Herbert Eldredge. Captain Kelley was appointed keeper of the new Monomoy Point Station in August, 1902,

CAPT. JOSEPH C. KELLEY, KEEPER OF MONOMOY POINT STATION.

although the station was not manned until Oct. 30, 1902. Captain Kelley has the distinction of being the youngest life-saving station keeper on Cape Cod, if not in the United States, having been honored with the appointment of keeper of the Monomoy Point Station when he was but twenty-nine years of age.

When a young man he was a boatman and fisherman along the

shores of Cape Cod, and later became a coastwise sailor. He became accustomed to the perils incident to the work of boating along the shores of the Cape, and skilled in handling boats in the roughest water at an early age. At the Peaked Hill Bars Station under the veteran seafighter, Captain Cook, Surfman Captain Kelley received a most thorough drilling in the work of life saving, which proved of untold benefit to him when he joined the Chatham Station, and better prepared him for the responsible position he now occupies. At the Chatham Station under Captain Eldredge, Captain Kelley was No. 1 surfman. He assisted at all the wrecks that occurred along the shore there for nearly five years, demonstrating his ability to cope with the most stupendous problems of life saving. Captain Kelley has a

THE HORSES THAT ARE KEPT ON DUTY AT MONOMOY POINT STATION.

selected crew of experienced and fearless surfmen, who in the brief history of the station have proven themselves equal to every emergency that has arisen.

Five disasters occurred on the shoals near the station within as many weeks after the station was manned, and in every case the vessels were saved and not a life was lost. Captain Kelley married Chestena Batchelder.

MONOMOY POINT STATION CREW.

The No. 1 surfman is Joseph D. Bloomer. He was born in Prince Edward Island in 1857, and has been in the life-saving service since Oct. 1, 1902. Surfman Bloomer followed the sea in one capacity or another since he was a boy. For five years he was engaged in trading between Portland and the West Indies Islands. Upon coming to

Cape Cod he took up his residence in Chatham, and for the past twenty-five years he has been a boatman, fisherman, anchor dragger, and wrecker on the shoals off Monomoy. Before entering the life-saving service as a regular surfman, he had substituted at the Chatham and Monomoy Stations, and was well used to the duties of a surfman. The rips and shoals off Monomoy are all familiar to Surfman Bloomer. During the twenty-five years that he has spent in that region he assisted at all the wrecks that took place near there, and was one of the

OBED H. SHIVERICK.   JOHN E. ELLIS.   JOSEPH D. BLOOMER.   CAPTAIN KELLEY.
RICHARD E. RYDER.   CHARLES G. HAMILTON.   REUBEN W. ELDREDGE.   EDWIN L. CLARK.

MONOMOY POINT CREW.

best-known Monomoy wreckers so-called. Skilled in the art of boating, with a thorough knowledge of the shoals along the shores of Cape Cod, Surfman Bloomer has few equals as a life saver. He married Adeline Bloomer.

The No. 2 surfman is John E. Ellis. He was born in West Harwich in 1874, and entered the life-saving service when this station was manned Oct. 1, 1902. Surfman Ellis followed the sea from the time

The Life Savers of Cape Cod.   131

that he was a boy until he joined the life-saving service. He engaged in steamboating for a few years, and later made a great number of trips on barges from the middle Atlantic ports around Cape Cod. He spent several years boating and fishing on the shoals off Monomoy, and is a skilled boatman and a fearless life saver. He married Lilian M. Ashley.

The No. 3 surfman is Obed H. Shiverick. He was born in Dennis in 1867, and entered the life-saving service when this station was manned.

Surfman Shiverick went to sea when a small boy, his first trip being to the Grand Banks. He was a fisherman for a number of years, when he joined the crew of the Cross Rip Lightship under Captain Jorgensen, and for four years was a member of the Nantucket Shoals Lightship, also under Captain Jorgensen, going with the veteran captain when he took charge of that floating beacon. Surfman Shiverick has had a wide and varied experience on the water. He is familiar with the rips and shoals along the shores of Cape Cod, is a skilled boatman, and a brave and efficient life saver. He married Sadie McQuarrie, and is the father of two daughters.

The No. 4 surfman is Edwin L. Clark. He was born in Chatham in 1876, and has been in the life-saving service since Oct. 1, 1902. Surfman Clark followed the sea from a boy. For a number of years he engaged in barge towing around Cape Cod, and later joined the crew of the Shovelful Lightship, where he remained one year. At different periods for two years he substituted at the Monomoy Station, under the late Captain Eldredge. He is well accustomed to the hardships incident to a surfman's life, skilled in the art of handling boats, and is an able life saver. He married Minnie B. West, and is the father of a daughter.

The No. 5 surfman is Reuben W. Eldredge. He was born in South Dennis in 1864, and entered the life-saving service when this station was manned. Surfman Eldredge followed the sea from a boy. For ten successive years he went cod-fishing to the Grand Banks. While fishing on the banks one season he lost track of his vessel during a thick fog, and was tossed about in an open dory for five days without food or water. He was finally picked up in an unconscious condition by a French fishing vessel, and put aboard his own vessel. He recovered in a short time, and despite the terrible suffering through which he passed, continued to go to the "banks" for several years. Later he became a coastwise sailor, and was also a member of the crew of the steamer *City of Macon* for some time.

Surfman Eldredge, after giving up going to sea, became a fisherman and wrecker along the shores of Monomoy. He also substituted at the Chatham Station under the late Captain Eldredge. He is perfectly at home in a boat under any and all conditions of wind or weather. The sea has no terrors for him, and he is inured to the hardships and perils of a life saver's life. He married Alice D. Young, and is the father of a son.

The No. 6 surfman is Joseph Christie. He was born in Scotland, is thirty-one years of age, and has been in the life-saving service since this station was manned. Surfman Christie was a boatman and fisherman for a number of years, and also served as substitute at the Cuttyhunk Life-Saving Station. He served in the United States Navy in the war with Spain. He married Lizzie Jackson. Surfman Christie is at present on sick leave, on account of injuries received in the performance of his duty.

The No. 7 surfman is John E. Ryder. He was born in Chatham in 1879, and has been in the life-saving service two years. He is the winter man, so called. During the summer season Surfman Ryder is stationed at the City Point Station, South Boston. Before entering the service he was a boatman and fisherman along the coast of Cape Cod, becoming familiar with the handling of boats in the surf, and acquiring a knowledge of the rips and shoals that abound there. He is an expert boatman and a brave and hardy life saver.

Surfman Charles G. Hamilton, who is substituting for Surfman Christie, joined the crew on Dec. 1, 1902. He was born in Chatham in 1859. He has been a boatman, lobsterman, fisherman, and wrecker off Monomoy for nearly twenty years. For the past fifteen years he has lived on Monomoy Point, and has assisted at nearly all the wrecks that have occurred in that vicinity during that time. He is a well-known wrecker, who knows the location of every rip and shoal in the region about Monomoy.

He was also a grand banker, a coastwise sailor, and engaged in steamboating around the Cape. He is thoroughly accustomed to the perils of the sea, and is an expert boatman and a fearless life saver. He married Etta Batchelder.

THE MONOMOY DISASTER.

When the late Capt. Marshall W. Eldredge was appointed keeper, Captain Ellis was his No. 1 surfman. Captain Ellis served as No. 1 surfman until May 1, 1902, when he was appointed keeper to succeed his late captain, whose life was given up in an heroic attempt to rescue an imperiled crew. Captain Ellis married Aureilla M. Cahoon, and is the father of one son. The story of the terrible tragedy in which Captain Eldredge and six members of his crew, together with five persons whom they had taken from the stranded barge *Wadena*, perished, is best told by the sole survivor, Captain Ellis, and is as follows: —

The Life Savers of Cape Cod. 133

"On Tuesday, March 11, 1902, about one o'clock A. M. the schooner barge *Wadena* stranded during a northeast gale and heavy sea on the Shovelful Shoal, off the southern end of Monomoy Island. The crew were rescued by our station crew. The barge remained on the shoal without showing any signs of going to pieces, and wreckers were engaged in lightering her cargo of coal. On the night of March 16 the weather became threatening, and all except five of the persons engaged in lightering the cargo were taken ashore from the barge by the tug *Peter Smith*, which was in the employ of the owners of the barge.

"Shortly before eight o'clock on the morning of March 17 one of the patrolmen from our station reported that the *Wadena* appeared to

BARGES WADENA AND FITZPATRICK STRANDED ON SHOALS AT MONOMOY.

Wadena in foreground. In attempting to take an imperiled crew off the *Wadena*, Captain Eldredge and six of his crew of life savers perished, together with the crew of the barge, five in number. March 17, 1902.

be in no immediate danger, but later Captain Eldredge received a message from Hyannis, inquiring whether everything was all right with the men aboard the barge. Up to this time no one at the station was aware that any persons had remained on the barge over night.

"Upon the receipt of this inquiry Captain Eldredge, putting on his hip boots and oil clothes, set out for the end of the Point, where he could personally ascertain the conditions.

"Arriving there he found that the barge was flying a signal of distress. He at once telephoned me, as I was the No. 1 man at the station, directing me to launch the surf-boat from the inside of the beach, and with the crew pull down to the Point. About two and one-half miles south of the station we took Captain Eldredge aboard and I gave him the steering oar.

"The wind was fresh from the southeast and there was a heavy sea running, but all the crew were of the opinion that the condition of the barge *Wadena* was not perilous, as she seemed to be sound and lying easy.

"Captain Eldredge decided to pull around the Point to the barge. At certain places on the shoals the sea was especially rough, and some water was shipped on the way out to the distressed craft, but without

DRILL OF THE MONOMOY CREW, SHORTLY BEFORE THE DISASTER
IN WHICH SEVEN OF THE CREW PERISHED.

any trouble we succeeded in bringing our surf-boat under the lee of the barge just abaft the forerigging, the only place where it was practical to go alongside.

"As soon as we got alongside the barge a line was thrown aboard and quickly made fast by the persons on board. The persons on board the barge were all excited and wanted us to take them ashore as soon as we could. Captain Eldredge, without a moment's delay, when he found out the number of persons on board the barge and their desire to be taken ashore, directed them to get into the surf-boat.

"The seas were breaking heavily around the stern of the barge, and there was little room for operations in the smooth water, and the rail of the barge was twelve or thirteen feet above the surf-boat. Four of the five men lowered themselves over the side of the barge, one at a time, into the surf-boat, without mishap, by means of a rope, but the captain of the barge, who was a big, heavy man, let go his hold when part way down and dropped into the boat with such force as to break the after thwart. All five being safely in the boat, two were placed forward, two aft, and one amidships, and told to sit quietly and keep close down in the bottom of the boat.

"In order to get away from the barge quickly, the painter was cut, by orders of Captain Eldredge, and the surf-boat was at once shoved off. In order to clear the line of breakers that extended from the stern of the barge so that we could lay a good course for the shore, a part of the surfmen were backing hard on the port oars, while the others gave way with full power on the starboard side. Before we could get the boat turned around a big wave struck us with fearful force, and quite a lot of water poured into the surf-boat.

"Captain Eldredge stood in the stern of the boat with the steering oar in his hand giving his orders, and the surfmen stuck to their posts.

"As soon as the water came into the boat, the rescued men jumped up, and becoming panic-stricken, threw their arms about the necks of the surfmen so that none of us could use our oars. The seas, one after another, struck us, and the boat, filling with water, turned bottom up, throwing us all into the raging sea. The seas kept striking us after the boat upset, and we were soon in among the heaviest breakers. Twice we righted the boat, but the seas which struck her before we could get into her capsized her each time.

"After righting the boat twice, our strength was fast leaving us, and we all knew that we could not survive long without assistance. The five men that we had taken off the barge were the first to be swept off the overturned boat and to perish before our eyes. They did not regain a hold of the boat after she turned over the first time, and were quickly swept to death.

"All of us clung to the boat, giving each other all the encouragement that we could. Surfman Chase was the first one of our crew to perish, then Nickerson and Small were swept to death. Captain Eldredge, Surfmen Kendrick, Foye and Rogers and myself still managed to hold to the boat. Every sea which struck the boat swept completely over us, almost smothering us. Kendrick was the next one of our crew to perish, and poor Foye soon followed him. Captain Eldredge and Surfman Rogers and myself were the only ones left, and we expected that we, too, would soon share the fate of our comrades.

"Rogers was clinging to the boat about amidships, while Captain Eldredge and myself were holding on near the stern. Captain Eldredge called to me to help him to get a better hold, and I managed to pull him on to the bottom of the boat, when a sea struck us and washed us both off. I managed to regain a hold on the bottom of the boat, and looking around for Captain Eldredge, I saw that he was holding on to the spar and sail which had drifted from underneath the boat, but was still fast to it. The seas were washing me off the boat continually at this time, and when I last saw our brave captain, he was drifting away from the boat, holding on to the spar and sail.

"My strength was fast going, and when poor Rogers begged me to help him climb further up onto the boat, the only thing I could do

CHURCH AT ORLEANS WHERE MEMORIAL SERVICES WERE HELD FOR LOST MONOMOY CREW.

was to tell him that we were drifting towards the beach, and that help would soon be at hand and to hold on.

"Rogers had lost his strength, however, and failing to get a more secure place on the bottom of the boat, feebly moaning, 'I have got to go,' he fell off the boat and sank beneath the waters.

"I was now alone on the bottom of the boat, and seeing that the center board had slipped part way out, I managed to get hold of it, and holding it with one hand succeeded in getting my oil clothes, undercoat, vest, and boots off.

"By that time the overturned boat had drifted down over the shoals in the direction of the barge *Fitzpatrick*, which was also stranded on the shoals, and when I sighted the craft I waved my hand as a signal for help. I soon saw those on the barge fling a dory over the side into the water, but could see nothing more of the dory after that on account of the mist and high sea until it hove in sight with a man in it rowing towards me. The man in the dory was brave Capt. Elmer F. Mayo. He ran the dory alongside of me, and with his help I got into the boat. I was so used up that I was speechless, and all that I could do was to kneel in the bottom of the boat and hold on to the thwarts. To land in the dory through the surf was a perilous undertaking, but Mayo, who is a skilled boatman, carefully picked his way over the rips and headed his little boat for the shore.

"Surfman Bloomer of our station, who had been left ashore, had walked down to the Point to assist Captain Eldredge and crew in landing, and when he saw Mayo fighting his way through the breakers, he ran down into the surf, seized the little boat, and helped Mayo to land safely.

"Bloomer was told of the terrible tragedy by Captain Mayo, as I was unable to speak at the time. As I have often said, ' If the persons we took off the barge had kept quiet as we told them to, all hands would have been landed in safety.'"

Seth. L. Ellis
Keeper, Monomoy L. S. Station

CAPT. ELMER F. MAYO.

Capt. Elmer F. Mayo, "The Hero of Monomoy," was born in Chatham, and is forty years of age. From boyhood he has been a boatman, fisherman, anchor dragger, a substitute at the life-saving stations on Cape Cod, and wrecker along the shores near Monomoy, and is well accustomed to the perils and rigors incident to work of that kind.

Among the boatmen and wreckers along the Chatham and Monomoy shores he has always been regarded as an A No. 1 boatman, skilled in the art and science of handling boats in the surf, and absolutely fearless. His father was the first keeper of the Chatham Station.

Upon the discovery of gold in the Klondike region a few years ago, Mayo joined a party of prospectors, and went to the Copper River country. He remained there but a short time, returning to Cape Cod and resuming his former occupation.

At the time of the Monomoy disaster, he was on board the barge *Fitzpatrick*, near by the stranded barge *Wadena*, in company with Captain Mallows of Chatham, and the captain of the barge.

The *Fitzpatrick* had stranded at the time the *Wadena* went on the shoals, and Mayo and Mallows were aboard arranging to float the craft. They had remained on board the *Fitzpatrick* over night, the same as those on board the *Wadena*, so as to be on hand early in the morning to begin the work.

There was a small fourteen-foot dory alongside the *Fitzpatrick*, and the night before the fatal disaster, the wind freshening up, Mayo

CAPT. ELMER F. MAYO, THE HERO OF MONOMOY, AND SURFMAN ELLIS, WHOM HE RESCUED.
Captain Mayo standing.

hauled the dory aboard, made some thole pins, and got a pair of oars ready for use should bad weather oblige them to go ashore.

The oars were too long for the small craft, and Mayo cut a piece off each of them. The wind blew a gale during the night preceding the disaster, and there was considerable rough water around the barge the next morning. The craft was not leaking, however, and there seemed no cause for alarm. A thick fog swept in over the shoals in the morning, hiding the stranded sister barge *Wadena* from the view of those on the *Fitzpatrick*, and they were in ignorance of the fact that a signal of distress was flying in her rigging.

The first intimation that Mayo and Mallows had that a terrible tragedy had been enacted within a short distance of them was when the overturned life-boat, with the sole survivor of the Monomoy life-saving crew, Surfman Ellis, clinging to it, was seen drifting out over the shoals.

At the sight of the life-boat with a surfman clinging to it, both Mayo and Mallows knew that a terrible disaster had happened. Mayo

FOURTEEN-FOOT DORY USED BY CAPT. ELMER F. MAYO, IN RESCUING SURFMAN ELLIS.

in an instant threw off all his clothing except his underclothes, and while Mallows entreated him not to go, telling him he believed that to attempt to reach the overturned life-boat would cost him his life, Mayo grabbed the dory, threw it into the raging sea, and slid down a rope from the barge into the frail craft.

With the improvised thole pins and the long oars, with handles so large that he could hardly grasp them, Mayo had a fearful struggle in preventing the dory from being swamped by the seas.

With a strong and steady stroke, and energy born of desperation, he kept the little boat head to the sea, sending her along with marvelous speed. Within a short time he was within hailing distance of the man on the bottom of the life-boat. Surfman Ellis saw the boat as it was thrown from the barge, but in the fog had lost sight of it. Mayo, however, had kept the overturned life-boat within sight all the time, and as soon as he got within hailing distance he shouted to Ellis, whom he then recognized, to hold on!

It was a hazardous task to take Ellis from the bottom of the life-boat, but both Mayo and Ellis were skilled in that kind of work, and it was successfully accomplished. To land on the beach through the surf would be attended with greater peril, but Mayo knew that Ellis must have immediate treatment, and after placing him in the bottom of the boat, he headed the dory straight for the shore. The fog still hung over the waters, and it was solely from his thorough knowledge

THE MONOMOY SURF-BOAT.

of the waters about that region that Mayo was able to avoid the myriads of shoals and rips, and guide the boat to a point on the beach where it would be possible to land. Surfman Bloomer, of the Monomoy Station, who had walked down the beach, saw the boat headed for the beach, and running down, got there just in time to assist Mayo in landing.

Both the United States Government and the Massachusetts Humane Society recognized this great heroic act of Captain Mayo, and awarded him medals. The committee having charge of the Monomoy Fund also presented him with a portion of the money received by them, in recognition of his heroism in rescuing Surfman Ellis from a watery grave.

Captain Mayo married Mrs. Priscilla Nye.

The late Capt. Isaac Green Fisher, keeper of the Wood End Station, was born in Truro in 1838, and was the son of Caleb and Mary G. Fisher, of that town. For twenty years he was keeper of the Peaked Hill Bars and Wood End Life-Saving stations, and was known the country over as a wondrous surf-fighter and saver of human life. Prior to his entering the life-saving service he had been engaged in whaling for a number of years, and won distinction in that skilled work by his fearlessness and marvelous dexterity with the steering oar.

As keeper of the dangerous Peaked Hill Bars Station, Captain Fisher rescued hundreds of shipwrecked seafarers, and assisted a countless number of stranded crafts to places of safety. He also assisted at nearly all the wrecks that took place at the stations along the back of the Cape, adjoining the Peaked Hill Bars Station.

He was retired from the service at his own request on account of physical disability, June 14, 1901, and died September 18 following.

THE LATE CAPT. ISAAC G. FISHER AND HIS CREW OF SURF FIGHTERS.

The Life Savers of Cape Cod.

RELATIVE POSITIONS OF MEN WHILE PLACING APPARATUS.

POSITION OF LIFE SAVERS WHEN SHOT LINE IS BENT TO WHIP.

HAULING OFF WHIP.
FULL CREW OF LIFE SAVERS PRACTICING WITH BREECHES-BUOY.

The Life Savers of Cape Cod. 143

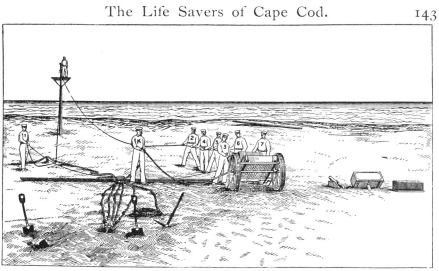

HAULING OFF THE HAWSER.

RAISING THE CROTCH.

MAN THE LEE WHIP. HAUL OFF.

144   The Life Savers of Cape Cod.

MAN WEATHER WHIP.   HAUL ASHORE.

In Memoriam.

To the memory of the heroes who gave up their lives in their devotion to duty.

    CAPT. MARSHALL N. ELDREDGE.
    SURFMAN ELIJAH KENDRICK.
    SURFMAN ISAAC T. FOY.
    SURFMAN VALENTINE D. NICKERSON.
    SURFMAN OSBORNE CHASE.
    SURFMAN EDGAR C. SMALL.
    SURFMAN ARTHUR ROGERS.
        — Monomoy, March 17, 1902.

    CAPT. DAVID H. ATKINS.
    SURFMAN FRANK MAYO.
    SURFMAN ELISHA TAYLOR.
        — Peaked Hill Bars, Nov. 30, 1880.

HORACE S. CROWELL,

Dealer, Broker, and Agent

SEASHORE ESTATES

216 Washington St., S. Cor. State St., Boston.

Telephone 1290 Main. W. U. Cable Address, "Crowe."

DEVELOPMENT, IMPROVEMENT, AND CARE OF ESTATES
A SPECIALTY.

OPEN DURING SUMMER SEASON

SMALL'S PHOTOGRAPHIC STUDIO

BUZZARD'S BAY, MASS.

Artistic Photographs in Platinum

NOVELTIES

Carbon Photographs on Wood, Leather, Porcelain, and Glass

TELEPHONE CONNECTIONS

JOHN ADAMS

Staple and Fancy Groceries

Meats and Provisions

COMMERCIAL STREET
PROVINCETOWN, MASS.

CAMPBELL'S
Livery and Boarding Stable

CARRIAGES FOR ALL OCCASIONS

We furnish careful drivers to accompany tourists to the Life-Saving Stations and all other points of interest

CONNECTED BY TELEPHONE

PROVINCETOWN, - - - MASS.

HOTEL ARAGON

MIDDLEBORO, MASS.

Heated by Steam   Electric Lights

Guests are assured of every
Comfort and Convenience

J. H. DALTON, *Manager*

Eldredge Bros.

LIVERY AND BOARDING STABLE

ORLEANS, MASS.

We furnish carriages for all occasions. Tourists taken to the Life-Saving Stations and all places of interest.

CONNECTED BY LONG DISTANCE TELEPHONE

"The Eagleston Shop"

HYANNIS, MASS.

Furniture and Fitments

China, Pottery and Rugs

For Summer Homes

HYANNIS, MASS.

HOTEL PILGRIM

PLYMOUTH, MASS.

Remodeled and Refurnished by New Owners

Will Open June 10, 1903

Improvements made this year include:

- Enlargement of Office
- Enlargement of Dining Room
- New Music Hall, Open Fireplace
- New Private and Public Baths
- New Ladies' Lavatory
- New Plumbing throughout
- Electric Lights
- New Billiard and Amusement Parlors
- New Carpets and Furniture
- New Porte Cochere
- New Sun Parlor
- New Bath Houses on the Beach
- New Landing Float for Boats
- Sail Boats, Experienced Skippers
- Row Boats
- Fishing Facilities
- A Good Stable

THE TABLE AND SERVICE WILL BE OF A HIGH ORDER

Our Illustrated Circular will be mailed on application

Address,

A. B. DAVIS, *Manager*

N. B. Until June 1 the manager may be seen on Saturdays from 9 a. m. to 4 p. m. at International Hotel and Tourist Bureau, 147 Summer Street, Boston.

ATLANTIC HOUSE

FRANK SMITH, Prop'r

Masonic Court, off Commercial Street

PROVINCETOWN, MASS.

OPEN ALL THE YEAR

Huyler's
Chocolates.

Cigars,
Imported and Domestic.

ADAMS, Pharmacist,

Opposite Post Office,
Provincetown, Mass.

Prescriptions
a
Specialty.

Ice-cold
Soda,
Fruit Flavors.

The Up-to-date Pharmacy.

HEATED BY STEAM   LIGHTED BY GAS

IYANOUGH HOUSE

HYANNIS, MASS.

T. H. SOULE, Jr., Prop'r

FIRST-CLASS LIVERY STABLE CONNECTED

S. L. HAMLIN

Staple and Fancy Groceries

THE LARGEST STORE
AND THE LARGEST STOCK
OF GROCERIES ON CAPE COD

FALMOUTH, MASS.

Branch Stores at Falmouth Heights and Teaticket

BOSTON BRANCH CLOTHING STORE

Clothiers, Hatters, and Outfitters

For Ladies, Gentlemen, Misses, and Children.

SATISFACTION GUARANTEED
or money refunded.

BOSTON BRANCH CLOTHING STORE,

JOHN S. ARENOVSKI, Proprietor and Manager,

Main Street, - - - FALMOUTH, MASS.

JOHN H. CROCKER

DEALER IN

SEASHORE ESTATES

FALMOUTH, MASS.

Grower of choice Cape Cod
CRANBERRIES

PATRONIZE THE

Boston and Hyannis Express

Forwarders of goods of all descriptions to all points in the United States at the lowest rates.

DAILY MESSENGER FROM HYANNIS TO BOSTON.

We are better prepared than any other express to handle Household Goods, Groceries, Lumber, Boats, and heavy goods at low rates for Hyannis, Hyannisport, Sea Side Park, Craigville, Centreville, Osterville, Hyannis Park, West Yarmouth, Englewood Beach, and South Yarmouth.

General Office, 105 Arch Street, Boston.

Telephone Main 906.   W. F. ORMSBY, Manager.

ORMSBY'S TRANSFER

Furnishes the carriage service at Hyannis station for carrying passengers and baggage in Hyannis or to any of the nearby summer resorts.

REGULAR MAIL CARRIAGE TO HYANNISPORT.

Special Carriages or Hacks when ordered.

W. F. ORMSBY, Proprietor.

Telephone Connection.   HYANNIS, MASS.

A Number Of
SIGNIFICANT WRECKS

The following is a partial list of shipwrecks that happened around Cape Cod. The wrecks occured between the establishment of the United States Life Saving Service in 1871, and 1902, when this book was written. The Cape averaged about thirty shipwrecks each year. These included groundings in fog or storms, sinking, loss by fire and other various causes. Whenever there was a partial loss, the ship was sometimes pulled off to sail again. Most of the vessels listed were tragedies where one or more of the crew lost their lives.

Dec. 26, 1873: American Ship *Peruvian,* with cargo of sugar & tin, Captain Vannah and crew of 23, wrecked at Peaked Hill. Total loss, all hands lost.

May 4, 1875: Italian bark *Giovanni,* with cargo of brimstone, Captain Ferri and crew of 14, wrecked at Truro Highlands. Total loss, 1 saved.

Apr. 4, 1876: Schooner *Idabella,* with cargo of ice, Captain Fisher and crew of 5, wrecked at Pamet River Station. Total loss, 5 saved.

Jan. 17, 1877: Canadian Schooner *Perit,* with cargo of potatoes, Captain Chadrey and crew of 18, wrecked at Nauset Beach, Chatham. Total loss, crew saved.

Jan. 3, 1878: Schooner *J. G. Babcock,* with cargo of coal, Captain Babcock and crew of 6, wrecked at Nauset Beach, Eastham. Total loss, seven men lost.

Apr. 4, 1879: Schooner *Sarah J. Fort,* with cargo of coal, Captain Steelman and crew of 5, wrecked at Peaked Hill Bars. Total loss, two men lost.

Feb. 13, 1880: Schooner *Leander A. Knowles,* with cargo of ice, Captain Bassett and crew of 6, wrecked at Handkerchief Shoals. Total loss, crew saved.

Sept. 19, 1881: Brig *Clara J. Adams,* with cargo of ice, Captain Dow and crew of 7, wrecked at Peak Hill Bar. Total loss, crew saved.

Jan. 11, 1882: Schooner *A.F. Ames,* with cargo of iron, Captain Achorn and crew of 6, wrecked at Race Point. Total loss, crew saved.

Nov. 16, 1883: Schooner *Wm. F. Garrison,* with cargo of coal, Captain Steelman and crew of 5, wrecked at Mononoy Island. Total loss, crew saved.

Dec. 20, 1884: Schooner *Carrie M. Richardson,* with cargo of lime, Captain Holbrook and crew of 5, wrecked at Peaked Hill Bar. Total loss, crew saved.

Nov. 28, 1885: Schooner *Moses Webster,* with cargo of sugar, Captain Rhodes and crew of 7, wrecked at Monomoy. Total loss, crew saved.

Mar. 22, 1886: Brig *Emily T. Sheldon,* with cargo of ice, Captain Hays and crew of 7, wrecked at High Head, Truro. Total loss, crew saved.

Mar. 15, 1887: Schooner *J.H. Eells,* with cargo of iron, Captain Wallace and crew of 3, wrecked at Nauset, Eastham. Total lost, 2 men lost.

Mar. 28, 1888: English Steamer *Canonbury,* with cargo of sugar, Captain Mitchell and crew of 23, wrecked off Nantucket. Total loss, crew saved.

Sept. 14, 1889: Schooner *Phineas W. Sprague,* with cargo of coal, Captain Wilson and crew of 8, wrecked on Chatham Bar. Total loss, crew saved.

Feb. 16, 1890: Schooner *Katie J. Barrett,* with cargo of ice, Captain McLeod and crew of 8, wrecked at Nauset Beach, Eastham. Partial loss, crew saved.

Feb. 18, 1891: Schooner *Gardener G. Deering,* with cargo of coal, Captain Swain and crew of 8, wrecked at Sow & Pigs reef. Total loss, crew saved.

Nov. 16, 1892: Schooner *Storm King,* with cargo of coal, Captain Swayne and crew of 4, wrecked on Monomoy Island. Total loss, crew saved.

Dec. 5, 1893: British ship *Jason,* with cargo of jute, Captain McMillan and crew of 24, wrecked at Pamet River, Truro. Total loss, 24 men lost.

Feb. 12, 1894: Schooner *Fortuna,* with cargo of fish, Captain Greenlaw and a crew of 22, wrecked at Race Point, Provincetown. Total loss, 2 men lost.

Apr. 9, 1894: Bark *Belmont,* with cargo of sugar, Captain Hagan and crew of 8, wrecked at Beaked Hill Bars. Total loss, 6 men lost.

Jan. 5, 1895: Schooner *Job H. Jackson, Jr.,* with cargo of coal, Captain Whittier and a crew of 8, wrecked at Peaked Hill Bars. Total loss, crew saved.

May 6, 1896: Schooner *Daniel B. Fearing,* with cargo of coal, Captain Clifford and crew of 8, wrecked at Cahoons Hollow, Wellfleet. Total loss, crew saved.

Sept. 14, 1896: Italian Bark *Monte Tabor,* with cargo of salt, Captain Genero and crew of 11, wrecked at Peaked Hill Bars. Total loss, 5 men lost.

Dec. 23, 1896: Schooner *Calvin B. Orcutt,* with no cargo, Captain Pearce and crew of 7, wrecked off Chatham in storm. Total loss, crew all lost.

Oct. 21, 1897: Schooner *Nellie Lamper,* with cargo of piling, Captain McLean and crew of 6, wrecked off Nauset Beach, Eastham. Total loss, crew saved.

Sept. 20, 1898: Barkentine *Harriet S. Jackson,* with cargo of sulphur, Captain Veazie and crew of 7, wrecked at Monomoy. Total loss, crew saved.

Nov. 27, 1898: Steamer *Portland,* with cargo of passengers, Captain Blanchard, crew and passengers, ship foundered off Cape. 174 people all lost.

Nov. 27, 1898: Schooner *Lester A. Lewis,* with cargo of phosphate, Captain Kimball and crew of 4, wrecked in Provincetown Harbor. Total loss, crew all lost.

Nov. 27, 1898: Schooner *Jordan L. Mott,* with cargo of coal, Captain Dyer and crew of 4, wrecked off Wood End. Total loss, 1 man lost.

Nov. 27, 1898: Schooner *Albert L. Butler,* with a cargo of logwood, Captain Leland and crew of 7, wrecked at Peaked Hills Bars. Total loss, 6 men lost.

Nov. 27, 1898: Steamer *Fairfax,* with a cargo of cotton & merchandise, Captain Johnson and crew of 47, wrecked at Sow & Pigs reef. Total loss, crew saved.

May 3, 1899: Schooner *Robert Byron,* with cargo of lime, Captain Hart and crew of 3, wrecked Race Point, Provincetown. Total loss, crew saved.

June 22, 1900: Schooner *Isaac H. Tillyer,* with cargo of coal, Captain Norton and crew of 6, wrecked on Cuttyhunk Island. Total loss, crew saved.

Oct. 6, 1900: Schooner *Katie G. Robinson,* with cargo of coal, Captain Anderson and crew of 6, wrecked on Peaked Hill Bars. Total loss, crew saved.

Jan. 3, 1901: Canadian Schooner *Lily,* with cargo of coal, Captain Kerr and crew of 7, wrecked on Nauset Beach, Orleans. Total loss, crew saved.

Jan. 19, 1901: Schooner *George P. Davenport,* with cargo of coal, Captain McLeod and crew of 9, wrecked at Cuttyhunk Island. Total loss, crew saved.

Jan. 21, 1901: Schooner *Electa Bailey,* with cargo of ice, Captain Clay and crew of 5, wrecked at Chatham. Total loss, crew saved.

Nov. 7, 1901: Canadian Schooner *John S. Parker,* with cargo of lumber, Captain Ernst and crew of 5, wrecked at Orleans Beach. Total loss, crew saved.

Feb. 7, 1902: Schooner *Jennie C. May,* with cargo of coal, Captain Pearce and crew of 7, wrecked on Peaked Hill Bars. Total loss, crew saved.

Feb. 13, 1902: Schooner *Elsie M. Smith,* with cargo of fish, Captain Nickerson and crew of 17, wrecked at Orleans Beach. Total loss, 2 men lost.

Mar. 11, 1902: Barges *Wadena & Fitzpatrick,* with cargo of coal, Crew of 17, wrecked off Monomoy, *Wadena* loss total, 12 men lost during rescue.

Mar. 28, 1902: Steamer *Indian,* with general cargo, Captain Crowell and crew of 29, wrecked off Cuttyhunk, partial loss, crew rescued.

Sept. 18, 1902: Schooner *Dora Mathews,* with no cargo, Captain Bonsey and crew of 6, wrecked at Monomoy. Total loss, crew saved.